CLEVER
WAYS
— WITH —
Climbers

CLEVER WAYS
WITH
Climbers

JANE TAYLOR

WARD LOCK

A WARD LOCK BOOK

First published in this edition 1995
by Ward Lock
Wellington House
125 Strand
LONDON
WC2R 0BB

A Cassell Imprint

Originally published in hardback as *Creative Planting with Climbers* (1991)

Distributed in the United States
by Sterling Publishing Co., Inc.
387 Park Avenue South, New York, NY 10016–8810

Distributed in Australia
by Capricorn Link (Australia) Pty Ltd
2/13 Carrington Road, Castle Hill NSW 2154

A British Library Cataloguing in Publication Data block for this book may be
obtained from the British Library

ISBN 0 7063 7375 8

Typeset by RGM, The Mews, Birkdale Village, Southport, England
Printed and bound in Spain by Graficromo

Frontispiece
*'Albertine' is a favourite summer-flowering rambler rose, dating from the 1920s. Vigorous and
fragrant, she is as well adapted to the formality of this stone balustrade as to an informal, cottage
garden setting, sprawling over a fence or hedge or transforming a summerhouse.*

CONTENTS

PREFACE

CLIMBERS ARE THE OPPORTUNISTS of the plant world. They grow in spaces which would not support a tree or shrub, because they need so little elbow-room. They make their growth vertically instead, using neighbouring trees and shrubs to reach up towards the light. More rarely, they may clothe a rocky cliff or scramble over a bank. When the most natural way for climbers to grow is among, through and over other plants, why do so many people seem to think that you must have a wall to grow them?

A moment's reflection tells you that there are many more ways to grow climbers in the garden than on a wall. You can follow nature's lead and give each of your garden trees or your larger shrubs a companion climber. And that goes for hedges, too. More formally, you can erect tripods or stout poles, arches or pergolas, trellis screens or simple fences, to support your climbers, and yes, you can even grow climbers on your walls, alone or in company with wall shrubs.

All this means that in the same amount of space you can add a whole new dimension of flower, foliage, fruit and fragrance. For just like any other group of plants, climbers can offer all these. There are gaudy climbers, there are climbers with blooms of stylized formality, and there are those with the simple elegance of nature's untamed children. There are deciduous climbers and evergreen climbers; there are those that have their brief moment of glory and those that will never disgrace you. There are climbers with fragrant flowers, their perfume evoking memories, or simply filling the air and our hearts with sweetness. There are woody climbers, herbaceous climbers that go underground for the winter, and annuals or biennials that behave just like any other annual or biennial, except they climb. There are hardy climbers and tender ones, climbers for shade and climbers for sun, easy climbers and finicky ones that demand to be cossetted. There are climbers for small spaces and those that will make a take-over bid as soon as you plant them. And almost any climber, if you do not give it something to hold on to, will grow just as cheerfully sideways to cover the ground or make a low, spready bush.

J. T.

Opposite. *The golden hop,* Humulus lupulus *'Aureus', is a showy, hardy and easy herbaceous climber, ideal for quickly clothing a pergola or fence. It can also be grown through a large shrub. Its bold, lime-yellow leaves are striking among purple foliage, or can join other shades of green in a more restful setting.*

1
THE POTENTIAL
OF CLIMBERS

MOST PEOPLE WHO ARE making a garden think first of flowers. So, of course, does nature; for the flower is nature's way of making more plants. The magic of evolution that created so many ways a flower can be pollinated has given us such varied flower forms as the five-petalled single rose, the starry clematis, the pea-flowered trails of wisteria and the claw-like honeysuckle, the papery umbrella and narrow bell of *Rhodochiton* and the waxy high-shouldered elegance of *Lapageria*, the declamatory trumpets of *Campsis* and the foamy sprays of the climbing hydrangeas.

FLOWERING CLIMBERS

Man's endeavours have added the scrolled formality of the hybrid rose, the wide perfection of the large-flowered clematis, the vivid varied colours of bougainvillea. All the spectrum is there: white jasmine, clear yellow canary creeper, orange Chilean glory vine, scarlet trumpet honeysuckle, crimson rose, purple passion flower, pink perennial pea, mauve climbing monkshood, the near-blue of many clematis and the pure sky blue of plumbago.

There are flowers for all seasons, too. Summer is the high season: roses and honeysuckles, jasmine and passion flower, the climbing hydrangeas, and a host of less familiar climbers, are at their best in the longest days. Spring is scarcely less blessed, with wisteria and several of the clematis in bloom. There is, indeed, a clematis for virtually every month of the year. Autumn sees many of the southern hemisphere climbers still in bloom: the mutisias or climbing daisies, the Chilean glory vine, the climbing solanums and the Scottish flame flower.

CLIMBERS AS FOLIAGE PLANTS

With few exceptions, flowers are fleeting compared with the leaves that sustain the plant. Even a deciduous climber will be in leaf for longer than it is in flower, so foliage becomes an important element in the garden.

In cool temperate gardens, if you want an evergreen climber, it is likely to be an ivy, or perhaps a climbing euonymus. There are of course several evergreen climbers with attractive foliage and flowers as well, from *Clematis armandii* to the trachelospermums. Among deciduous climbers, the boldest leaves are borne by a vine, *Vitis coignetiae*, but *Actinidia chinensis*, the Chinese gooseberry, and *Aristolochia macrophylla*, the Dutchman's pipe, run it pretty close. The vine family makes a speciality of flaming autumn colours as well — the Virginia creeper and the Boston ivy, both residing in the genus *Parthenocissus*, as well as the true vines or *Vitis*.

There are several climbers with variegated foliage, from the frail *Ampelopsis brevipedunculata* 'Elegans' (another vine) to the magnificent forms of *Hedera colchica*, the Persian ivy. There are the netted honeysuckle, *Lonicera japonica* 'Aureo-reticulata', variegated jasmines, a pretty tricoloured form of *Trachelospermum jasminoides*, and a variegated hop which can be grown as an annual.

There are even a few climbers with coloured foliage: the teinturier grape with purple foliage and the dusty miller vine with grey, the grey-blue *Lonicera splendida*, the golden hop, and the burgundy-red winter foliage of the trachelospermums.

FRUITING CLIMBERS

Hardy climbers with edible fruits are not many. The Kiwi fruit is becoming more familiar as new varieties are introduced. Only in warm gardens will passion fruit mature, but in many gardens with a sunny wall, grapes could ripen.

Ornamental fruits are more common. *Ampelopsis brevipedunculata*, in a hot summer, will form clusters of bright turquoise berries. The fruits of *Billardiera longiflora* are deeper royal blue. Several climbing roses are valued in autumn, especially the musk roses, which bear great clusters of small, vivid hips. The climbing bittersweet, *Celastrus orbiculatus*, has sprays of fruits rather like the related spindleberries, but in orange and scarlet. The unusual schisandras bear clusters of bright red fruits. Somewhere between ornamental and edible come the sausage-shaped fruits of *Akebia* and *Lardizabala*, dark purple and pulpy.

If you count seedheads as fruits — which, botanically speaking, they are — several clematis qualify for inclusion. The silky, silvery-white wigs of the yellow lantern-flowered clematis and others are like superior old man's beard.

CLIMBERS FOR FRAGRANCE

And so to fragrance. It is surely no accident that of the five most popular hardy climbers — wisteria, rose, honeysuckle, jasmine, clematis — four are notable for their fragrance, so that one feels impelled to apologize for a honeysuckle or a rose without scent. Even among clematis, there are some that are fragrant: the vanilla-scented *Clematis armandii* and *C. montana*, the lemony *C. serratifolia* and *C. cirrhosa* to name a few. The perfume of honeysuckle and of jasmine is at its most eloquent in the evening, when it wafts far on the night air. The musk roses fling their amazing fruit scent with equal abandon by day and night; and wisteria is somehow a daytime scent, wholesome and fresh.

In spring, *Holboellia* and the related *Stauntonia* bear their modest but deliciously fragrant flowers, and the spicy-scented, chocolate-maroon cups of the akebias open. Summer is the season not only of the honeysuckles and jasmines but also of the hoya-like *Dregea sinensis* (*Wattakaka sinensis*), of the Chilean jasmine with its propeller-shaped flowers (it is related to the periwinkles, not the true jasmines) and of the trachelospermums.

2
MAKING THE MOST OF CLIMBERS

HOWEVER NATURAL IT MAY BE for climbers to grow up trees and through shrubs, it remains true that most people think first of walls as the natural place for their support in the garden. So it is with walls that I shall begin, followed by other artifices such as fences, trellises and tripods. This also acknowledges that in a brand new garden, there will not be convenient trees and shrubs to festoon with swags of roses or to garland with honeysuckle. Such romantic profusion can be achieved by other means, while you wait for your host trees to grow.

WALLS

Since it is only in the grandest establishments that the house is separated from the garden, I can say that every garden will have a wall, and often two, three or maybe even four, where climbers could grow: the walls of the house. Unfortunately, builders love to set houses in a plinth of paved or concreted pathways. Paving is not too much of a problem: you can lift a slab or two where you want to plant, dig out the rubble and rubbish beneath and refill with a rich and crumbly planting mixture, and tuck your climber in.

Concrete paths, however, are another and much worse matter. If you are able-bodied and energetic, you can dissipate lots of aggression by swinging a pick at the path until enough of it is broken up to make a bed for your plants. If you are not, may I suggest hiring a teenager? Fiddly weeding or planting seldom appeals to them, but the thought of earning money bashing a path to pieces may prove irresistible.

Whenever you plan to plant anything in a bed against your house walls, remember that the level of the soil must remain below that of the damp course, or you will have all sorts of problems indoors. If in doubt, ask the advice of a reput-

Opposite
Clematis and roses make a classic combination. Here 'Perle d'Azur', one of the finest of blue clematis, joins the clear pink climbing rose 'Coral Dawn', which blooms over a long season. If pink and blue do not appeal, try white on white, or a bold blend of purple clematis and yellow rose.

11

able builder or landscape consultant. A little expenditure at this stage could save heavy expense later.

Let us suppose, then, that you have banished your concrete path, excavated the rubble and subsoil, and replaced it with enriched soil (more about planting techniques, including soil preparation, in a later chapter). What are the next considerations?

However tempting the image of a cottage wreathed in honeysuckle and roses, pause a moment to ask yourself if this is really what you want. Remember that roses and honeysuckle, however beautiful in flower, are nothing to look at when *not* in flower; and that goes for clematis and wisteria, too. And roses, with few exceptions, are apt to fling out thorny arms to catch you unawares as you enter your own home.

I am assuming that you do not live in a fine scheduled building. If you do, you will probably want to leave its walls unadorned. If, like the huge majority of us, you do not, then your house will probably look the better for having its nakedness modestly clad. The best place to start is the front door, through which you often pass and where your visitors will receive their first impressions.

Comely climbers for key positions

There is a house I know where, many years ago, two trachelospermums were planted around the front door. Almost everything you could ask of a climber in this important position is embodied in the two species grown in cool-temperate gardens. Both *Trachelospermum jasminoides* and *T. asiaticum* are evergreen. Both are virtually self-clinging. Both look manicured with the minimum effort of pruning and training, and both have very fragrant flowers. They are not bone hardy in cold gardens but you cannot have everything, and with wall shelter they survive in many quite cold gardens. I will describe them in more detail later, for there are other climbers to consider here.

The trachelospermums are best on a sunny or semi-shaded wall. The evergreen climbing hydrangeas, though they flower more freely in sun, do very well even on dark walls, where their foliage is always comely. *Hydrangea serratifolia* and *Pileostegia viburnoides* both have frothy, creamy flowers, not the coloured mop-heads of many shrubby hydrangeas; they have good glossy foliage too. If you find the combination of green and cream or ivory too sober, then try running a plant of *Tropaeolum speciosum*, the Scottish flame flower, through them. This climbing nasturtium prefers a cool, shady spot.

Variegated foliage can be as bright as any flower, and climbers with variegated leaves will get a whole section to themselves. Meanwhile, for our front door climbers, one of the bold and beautiful ivies or the more vigorous climbing forms of *Euonymus fortunei* will look cheerful all year. They are self-clinging and easygoing. Some people assert that ivy will damage your walls. So long as the wall is sound, they will not; by keeping it dry, they may help to keep an old wall in good condition. Loose mortar may come away if you have to tear down well-rooted stems, but that is all.

If you are going to use a rose, a clematis, a wisteria or a honeysuckle in an important position where you will see it all the time, then you should discipline yourself to prune and train it scrupulously. This way it will at least look tidy when out of bloom. These climbers can also be combined with handsome wall shrubs, preferably evergreen, so that you have something comforting to look at in the off season. You can also combine two flowering climbers, either to extend the season — a rose following wisteria, for example — or to make a double impact in one season. The classic combination of this kind is rose plus clematis.

One of the nicest ways to use fragrant climbers such as these is around a window that you sit by in summer. Then, whenever the window is open, the perfume of your climber will waft into the room as well as filling the garden. The climbers which are at their most fragrant after dusk are romantic choices for a window planting: honeysuckle and jasmine.

Cottages, or cottage-style houses, often have a porch around the front door. To enhance the cottage atmosphere, you could plant a jasmine or honeysuckle to wreath the porch, and accept that for much of the year it will be a tangle of leaves or of bare stems.

The grandest equivalent of a jasmine porch, for houses with sufficient height and span, is an immaculately trained wisteria. In its short season, nothing looks more splendid, but you need to be confident of remaining for several decades in your house if you decide to plant a wisteria with those great curtains of lilac tresses in mind. You must be disciplined enough to undertake the twice-yearly pruning and training needed if your wisteria is to develop into a properly disposed adornment for your home, and to stay that way.

Do think hard, then, before choosing a climber for a key wall position. The wrong one may be a reproach to you for eleven months of every year. The right one should give a little frisson of pleasure each time you pass through your front door. Remember, you still have all the other walls of your house for the romantic but less dressy climbers you want to grow. You may have other walls as well: a shed or outhouse, a boundary wall, a summerhouse. They can all be made to shelter a climber. A cottage garden I know has the village post-box, one of those big old-fashioned ones, set in the road-side fence; someone, years ago, planted a honeysuckle against it, and every summer the post-box is half hidden among the perfumed clusters of maroon and cream flowers.

Sunny or shady walls

The aspect of your wall will affect the choice of climber. On an ordinarily sunny wall most climbers will do well, especially those that we choose for their flowers, but on a shaded wall, so long as it is not too dark, many roses and clematis will also do well. Several honeysuckles do better in cooler places, especially the glorious, but scentless, *Lonicera tragophylla*. All the climbing hydrangeas, the deciduous ones as well as the evergreen, do well on part-shaded walls, and so do several vines.

The hottest and most sheltered walls should be reserved for less hardy climbers, and those that need a good baking to flower well. In the first category are, for example, the passion flowers; the passion-flower look-alike *Clematis florida* 'Sieboldii'; the Chilean jasmine; the Banksian rose, and others. If you hope for ripe fruits, grape vines need plenty of sun; and for a good crop of those spectacular scarlet trumpets, so do all the *Campsis* and their *Bignonia* relatives. A wall that gets only the afternoon sun, so long as it is sheltered, will do for the slightly tender climbers; those that are winter-hardy, yet need long hot summers to flower well, should be given a wall facing right into the midday sun, at least in climates where summers are often overcast or cool.

The way they climb may matter, too. Generally, it is easier to cope with self-clinging or with tendril climbers than with twining ones, on a wall. Later, in a chapter on the practicalities of growing climbers, I will look at the ways climbers attach themselves, and how we can help them with various methods of support in the garden. Talking of support, do not forget that climbers can help to conceal drainpipes or other utilitarian excrescences.

FENCES FOR CLIMBERS

Fences, like walls, can be covered by a self-clinging climber such as an ivy or a euonymus. I mean a reasonably solid fence, larch-lap for example; but also chain-link, which is efficient but ugly. Plant some ivies along its length and transform it into a fedge, a strip of greenery that looks like a hedge but takes up a fraction of its space, laterally.

Ranch fences and other post-and-rail types can well support climbers (Figs. 1 & 2). A rustic rail fence wreathed in an abundance of rose blossom, or set with the great dinner-plate leaves of *Vitis coignetiae*, could make an internal division in your garden or a visually arresting boundary. The more supple climbers, that hold on by twining stems, are generally useful on fences. Some twiners, notoriously the more vigorous honeysuckles, can actually strangle a living host with their encircling stems; there is no such danger on a fence.

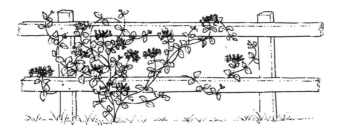

Fig. 1.   Honeysuckle on a post and rail fence.

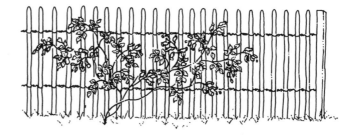

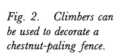

Fig. 2.   Climbers can be used to decorate a chestnut-paling fence.

A bright variegated ivy, Hedera helix *'Goldheart', gives support to the frail stems of the Scottish flame flower,* Tropaeolum speciosum, *on a half-shaded wall. The tropaeolum dies down in winter, leaving the ivy to brighten grey, chilly winter days. A more traditional way to grow the flame flower is on a clipped yew hedge.*

TRELLIS, PERGOLAS AND OTHER DEVICES

Trellis and screens are, in a sense, rather specialized fences. As the word screen implies, they may be intended to make a visual separation between two parts of the garden, or perhaps to conceal from view something outside the garden: anything from a nearby power station or factory to next door's washing line or carport. The word trellis implies something more open, less of a barrier to the eye, more of an ornamental suggestion of something beyond. Much the same may be true of an arch.

All three — arches, trellis and screens — can be decorated with climbers. More often than not, they are frankly artificial. They have, perhaps, a rather old-fashioned air to them, and that means that rather formal climbers suit them well: double-flowered roses rather than single, sweet peas in all their glorious colours, large-flowered clematis, climbers with coloured or variegated foliage (Fig. 3).

Of course, you may erect a trellis or an arch purely as a way of making room for more climbers, and in that case, the structure may be more functional than elegant. That is the time to smother it in a vigorous or leafy climber, so that as little of the support as possible can be seen. Provided the construction is strong

Fig. 3.   Ready-made metal garden arch half hidden under the luxuriant growth of rambler roses.

enough, you could even combine two climbers: a leafy concealing one such as a vine, with another chosen more for its flowers. There is scope for many exciting combinations here: a large-flowered, double mauve clematis or a passion flower through the teinturier grape with its dusky purple foliage, or *Lonicera caprifolium*, the early, cream-flowered honeysuckle, with a rambler rose to follow.

A pergola is something altogether grander (Fig. 4). It may be made wholly of wood, or of brick, tile or masonry pillars with timber cross-beams — scope for amateur bricklayers to try their skills, perhaps. It can be rustic or elegant; the choice will depend upon the surroundings and especially the dwelling house. A

Fig. 4.   A rather grand pergola with brick piers and wooden cross-beams, supporting a vine.

garden belonging to a cottage should, perhaps, not have a pergola at all; if it does, rusticity is more appropriate than elegance. With a stone-built cottage, round or square stone pillars with rough-cut beams will look better than all timber.

A Georgian-style brick house calls for a brick-pillared pergola, or one made of square-cut and planed timber. With the more anonymous architectural style of the houses that most of us live in, the degree of formality you allow yourself in the garden may be more important in your decision than the materials your house is built of. The essential, whichever style you choose, is that it should be of solid construction. Flimsy poles will never look right, but in any case will soon give under the weight of all but the most modest climbers.

Something close to the pergola in effect, though lacking the cross-beams, is the

Fig. 5.   Wooden pillars linked by ropes are an attractive way to display swags of rose blossom.

double row of pillars linked with stout ropes, to be decked with swags of blossom in summer (Fig. 5). This is a good choice if you live where it often rains, and where a fine day is one that is merely overcast, not wet. Here the shade of a pergola will be no blessing as it is in hotter, sunnier climes. And you will be spared, after rain, the ordeal of drips down your neck as you walk beneath your sodden roses or vines.

Wherever you have uprights and horizontals, whether over your head or not, you have scope for two kinds of climbers: shortish, often stiff-growing ones, to clothe the pillars, and vigorous, relaxed growers to reach the top of the uprights and cover the cross-beams. Now you need to bear in mind that most plants flower towards the light, so you may find your overhead climbers bearing all their flowers on top of the pergola where you cannot see them. You need kinds with nodding flowers such as certain roses or wisteria with its hanging trails.

A pergola will almost always look better if you plant with restraint, choosing just one, or perhaps two, kinds of climber for the cross-beams and a single kind, again, for the uprights. The repetition of few elements always carries more impact than a jumble of different shapes and colours. However, gardeners are often collectors, falling for this variety and that and wanting to pack more and more into

Fig. 6. A gazebo wreathed in wisteria.

the garden. If you must use your pergola to support several different climbing roses, for example, do at least try to make them all of one kind, rather than mixing large-flowered hybrid-tea types with informal single-flowered ramblers; and try to grade the colours. A progression from crimson through candy and pale pink to blush and white will look better than a kaleidoscope of colours.

If trellis and screens are for dividing the garden or hiding monstrosities, and pergolas for walking beneath in glad shade, arbours and gazebos are for sitting in (Fig. 6). A gazebo, the dictionary tells me, is 'a place whence a view may be had'. The view does not have to be distant, romantic hills or a dramatic coastline, agreeable though these may be to possess. It could be of a statue you have placed as a focal point; a fine specimen tree; a gate into a field, suggesting, though not revealing, wider spaces beyond. Whatever it may be, do not choose such densely leafy climbers that the view is soon hidden.

An arbour, by contrast, implies seclusion, so a thick curtain of foliage may be welcome to give the feel of a secret hideaway. This is the place to plant fragrant climbers so your idle hours pass filled with delight.

TRIPODS AND POLES

What, you may ask, has all this about pergolas and gazebos to do with me? I have only a tiny garden; where am I supposed to put my climbers?

How about setting some poles or tripods in your borders? They take little room, especially the poles; and you can use them to add height and colour in your borders with the least loss of planting space (Fig. 7). Among shrub roses, a climber such as *Clematis* 'Perle d'Azur' brings tones of almost pure blue, that are lacking in the roses. Some trails of the clematis can be allowed, or encouraged, to stray into the rose bushes. A honeysuckle that is tied in to a pole will usually flower with abandon, a pillar of fragrance. A bold-leaved variegated ivy will be a column of cheering colour in winter among the dereliction of your border plants, and a cooling contrast to bright flowers in summer.

Fig. 7. A wooden tripod adds height in the border, giving support to a jasmine.

On a tripod of sufficient height, you can even grow a rambling rose; not the most rampant, the big synstylae kinds that reach 9 m (30 ft) or more, but certainly the moderately vigorous varieties that are annually pruned after flowering.

A pyramid of trellis, in effect a more formal (and more expensive) variant on the simple tripod, is ideal for twining or tendril climbers, as there is more for them to hold on to than on a pole. A double row of pyramids could even make an alternative to a pergola, good — like the rope swags – in wetter climates where the overhead foliage is more of a drawback than a bonus.

Lighter structures of three or five bamboo canes, set in the ground wigwam fashion, can be used to support annual climbers to ring the changes in your borders. They can also be helpful as temporary supports for a climber that will ultimately inhabit a host shrub, while the shrub is maturing. If you find that you have not matched the vigour of the host and the climber so that the poor shrub risks being swamped, then a pole or tripod of more permanent nature can keep on taking much of the weight.

CLIMBERS IN CONTAINERS

Almost any plant will grow in a container, provided you look after it properly, and that is just as true of climbers. You would not, I hope, put a Kiftsgate rose in a tub; but there are plenty of climbing plants of more modest size that you could (Fig. 8).

On town-house balconies and in the little basement areas belonging to what real estate agents call garden apartments, all sorts of climbers grow very happily in urns, tubs or planters. All the favourites are there: honeysuckle, jasmine (especially the slightly tender, exotically perfumed *Jasminum polyanthum*), clematis, or the smaller roses. Sometimes they have been given their own trellis, set against the wall of the basement area; sometimes they wreath the balcony; sometimes they have shot up from below street level to deck the railings and delight passers by with their fragrance.

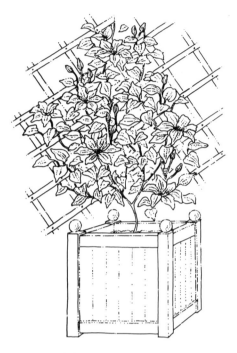

Fig. 8.   A formal planter of caisse de Versailles *style holds a clematis for summer flower, twining into trellis on the wall behind.*

Fig. 9.   A half-barrel with sweet peas on a cane wigwam and trailing Helichrysum.

Such arrangements translate very well to gardens out of town. Sometimes, despite what I said earlier about breaking up concrete paths, it may not be possible to make planting areas against your house walls. The answer is simple: set the climbers in tubs instead (Fig. 9). In a little courtyard I know, at the back of a country farmhouse, three half barrels are filled in spring with tulips or polyanthus; in summer, three canes make a lightweight tripod on which sweet peas grow. Their clear, bright colours are set off by the whitewashed walls behind and by the swirl of grey foliage of *Helichrysum petiolare* that shares the barrels with them.

Annual or herbaceous climbers have the advantage of retiring gracefully once they have done what you wanted of them, so you can tuck in pansies for winter and polyanthus for spring to keep your containers well dressed all year. All sorts of summer combinations are possible. Try, for example, the climbing nasturtium *Tropaeolum tuberosum* with the pale-leaved *Helichrysum petiolare* 'Limelight' and *Bidens ferulaefolia* with its lacy foliage and bright yellow lazy-daisy flowers. The violet bells of *Cobaea scandens* would combine with trailing, pink-flowered osteospermums. The sombre *Rhodochiton atrosanguineum* is enlivened by shell pink *Convolvulus elegantissimus*, which has finely cut silver foliage on twining stems. Its bindweed flowers are much smaller than the wide saucers of the morning glory, a splendid container climber which everyone admires for its rare colouring, in the form of *Ipomoea tricolor* 'Heavenly Blue', of pure turquoise.

Small-flowered clematis with *C. viticella* blood in them are best cut almost to ground level each winter. These, too, could be grown in a container, with either a wigwam of canes or, if your tub stands against a wall, a trellis to climb through in summer. Even quite a small container would suit the doll's house climbing rose 'Pompon de Paris', and you might plant at its feet the tiny double campanula 'Elizabeth Oliver' with full-petalled bells of pale china blue to contrast with the roses' sugar pink.

Just as your choice of pergola or gazebo, arbour or arch, should be in keeping with your house and garden style, so should containers. The half barrels in the little country courtyard look quite at home; by a neo-classical town house they would look absurdly rustic. The Ali Baba jars at Sissinghurst Castle in Kent, England, must have inspired many gardeners to plant a tumbling clematis in just such a tall, narrow-mouthed jar. There are plenty of handsome, weatherproofed terracotta containers on the market these days, or the reconstituted stone urns and planters that look surprisingly authentic. You can 'age' them by brushing over them a weak solution of liquid manure, or some sour milk; this will hasten the growth of lichens and take the raw newness off their colour.

If stone urns, even the reconstituted variety, are beyond your pocket, then you could even fall back on plastic. Here I think the plain, square or round, white or beige planters that honestly admit to being plastic look much better than the moulded synthetics which pretend to be stone. Filled with a mix of trailing and climbing plants, they will soon be half concealed, their hard edges lost in a softening skirt of foliage.

With imagination, almost anything can be turned into a plant container. I am distinctly unenthusiastic about old car tyres as planters, and old wheelbarrows have become a bit of a cliché. Even then, a real old wheelbarrow could be acceptable where a fake one that has never seen service carting weeds or manure would not. I have seen the basket of a delivery boy's bicycle effectively used. It was painted with the name of the nursery where the plants were grown, the owners having abandoned vegetables in favour of unusual ornamental plants, and was filled with a splendid mixture of soft coloured flowers and silvery foliage, including the climbing plumbago, *Plumbago auriculata*, with clusters of sky blue flowers, and the half climbing, silvery *Senecio vira-vira*. Because it was still on the bicycle, one of those robust, tall old black ones, there was plenty of room for the plants to tumble gracefully down as well as to reach upwards.

3
CLIMBERS IN HOST SHRUBS AND TREES

WHEN IT COMES TO MORE natural ways of growing climbers, it is easy to think that you need trees. Because most of today's small gardens have room for only one or two trees, their owners tend to think they have no room for climbers.

Happily, most of us have more room than we think. Any woody plant, shrub or tree, can host a climber. The only proviso is that you need to match the vigour of the shrub to its occupant. Thus, after only a few years, you may find you actually have more places to grow climbers than you can afford to fill.

CLIMBERS IN SHRUBS

This was brought home to me in a garden I made from a bare site, some years ago. Attracted by the small-flowered *Clematis viticella* hybrids, I discovered that there were eight or ten available in commerce, but I did not think I had eight or ten places to grow them, in a garden only five years old. So, pencil and notebook in hand, I walked the garden to see where they might go. I came back with fifty-two possibilities. *C.* 'Abundance', with its bright claret red blooms, could go on a patch of golden-leaved winter heather; *C.* 'Etoile Violette' in a silver willow; *C.* 'Purpurea Plena Elegans' joined the old purple moss rose *Rosa* 'William Lobb', two full-petalled, dusky violet flowers together; in a grey-leaved buddleia, *B.* 'Lochinch', I set the white, purple-margined and veined *C.* 'Venosa Violacea' — buddleias, like these clematis, are normally hard-pruned each year, so matching them was no problem. And so it went on, as we shall see when I come to write in more detail about clematis in a later chapter.

Finding so many more potential host shrubs than I had expected, I started devising combinations using other climbers as well. The golden hop was given a

Opposite
Rhododendrons, like other spring-flowering shrubs, can host an early clematis. The dainty, blue and white flowers of Clematis macropetala *contrast with the bold trusses of a pink rhododendron; later the silky wigs of the clematis seed heads will gleam against the dark rhododendron foliage.*

big purple berberis as support: rather a jazzy mixture, but always admired by visitors. The hop is very vigorous, but is herbaceous, so you simply yank out the dead topgrowth at the year's end. A stout pole to take some of the excess weight would have been a good idea, though.

Purple foliage is rare among climbers but quite common in shrubs. The dark *Cotinus coggygria* 'Royal Purple' made a flattering backdrop for the pink, tulip-shaped flowers of *Clematis* 'Duchess of Albany', while the brighter cherry pink 'Gravetye Beauty' found its way into the plum and glaucous foliage of *Rosa glauca* (*R. rubrifolia*). Stray clematis flowers bob up among the powder-blue fuzz of *Ceanothus* 'Gloire de Versailles' in the same border.

The spring-flowering *Clematis alpina*, with its blue lanterns, was led into the branches of *Physocarpus opulifolius* 'Luteus', which has bronzed young foliage maturing in summer to fresh chartreuse yellow. The blue lanterns also look charming with the single yellow flowers of *Kerria japonica* 'Guinea Gold'.

The winter jasmine — more of a scrambler than a climber — joined *Cotoneaster horizontalis*, the fishbone cotoneaster, and a Japanese quince on a shaded wall, for a cheering winter picture of yellow flowers, red berries and the large yellow fruits of the quince. To liven up the summer scene I added *Lonicera* 'Dropmore Scarlet', a vivid but scentless honeysuckle.

Roses as climbers will feature in a later chapter, but roses can also be hosts to other climbers. The taller shrub roses are the most suitable. In *Rosa moyseii* 'Geranium', which has Tudor-rose flowers of rich scarlet, I planted the climbing *Senecio scandens*, its masses of yellow daisies contrasting with the rose's orange, flask-shaped hips. A climber which dies partly down in winter, like this, or which can be hard pruned, like many clematis, is regarded as the most suitable to grow through roses.

Annual climbers are just as good for quick effect among shrubs as they are to do a rapid cover-up of an ugly chain-link fence. And using annual climbers, you can change your schemes each year much more easily. The canary creeper, *Tropaeolum peregrinum*, was my choice one year to decorate with its lemon nasturtium flowers the silvery *Hippophae rhamnoides* (sea buckthorn). The year after, I chose *Eccremo-carpus scaber*, the Chilean glory vine (a perennial which can be grown as an annual). The year after that, I chose subtle colours not bright: the violet bells of *Cobaea scandens*.

In gardens warm enough to grow *Abutilon vitifolium*, a shrubby or tree-like mallow with soft grey-green leaves and lavender or white saucer flowers, you should also succeed with *Solanum crispum* 'Glasnevin' as a free-standing scrambler. Combine the two, and you have a long succession of flowers, the first of the solanum's violet potato-flowers opening before the mallow has finished, and lasting until autumn.

Matching vigour need not mean thinking vertical all the time. Climbers are often just as happy sprawling sideways along a group of low shrubs, such as heathers, junipers, or even quite soft-wooded shrubs such as *Ballota pseudo-dictamnus*. In a garden I know, this velvety, grey-leaved plant is the background for *Clematis* 'Perle d'Azur', the ideal setting for its periwinkle blue blooms.

Some climbers can be used to fill gaps in your borders where early-flowering perennials like oriental poppies grow. The perennial pea, *Lathyrus latifolius*, has supple stems that can be kept clear of the poppies in their season and then brought forward to flower in their turn. *Tropaeolum tuberosum* performs the same trick of following on by making its growth with great rapidity from midsummer onwards; it can be trained horizontally on half-snapped peasticks, just as well as upwards.

The climbing monkshood, *Aconitum volubile*, mixes well with the big *Hydrangea paniculata* 'Tardiva', both flowering in autumn, or you could pair it with a shrub that flowers earlier, or with one that has attractive variegated foliage to set off the slate blue hooded flowers. Cream and green *Cornus alba* 'Elegantissima' would be a good choice. You will note that all three — monkshood, hydrangea and dogwood — enjoy similar conditions of cool, not too dry soil.

This aspect is, of course, just as important as matching the vigour of host and climber. However good you may think the combination will look, if the shrub wants cool moist soil in a shady spot and the climber insists on baking sun to perform, you are in for a disappointment. Most climbers, as we shall see, appreciate coolness at the root, as in their native haunts. The cool roots they will almost automatically get, if they are planted among shrubs, but they may not be suited in other ways if you are not mindful of their needs. Some must have full sun, others prefer dappled or even quite deep shade on their stems and leaves.

Climbers can do a wonderful job livening up shrubs that are drab once their flowers are over. Many of the old garden favourites have this failing; for example, forsythia, lilac, weigela, or mock orange, although indispensable in bloom, are best ignored for eleven months of the year, unless you decide to exploit them as supports for another plant.

Sometimes the way you have combined your shrubs might suggest a suitable climber. Say you have set the bridal wreath, *Spiraea arguta*, against a dark background of yew. White on deep green could be repeated later with a white clematis in the yew, a few trails leaning across into the spiraea as well. Perhaps you have admired the new *Caryopteris* × *clandonensis* 'Worcester Gold' in a nursery or on a trade stand at a flower show, and thought how well it would look with one of the blue junipers. At Burford House, Tenbury Wells, in England near the Welsh border, John Treasure has added a third component: a small-flowered clematis of near-blue, reclining on both the caryopteris and the juniper. Their habit of growth means that climbers are exceptionally good at this job of linking neighbouring plants to make a unified scheme.

Senecio vira-vira (better known as *S. leucostachys*) is half a weaver, half a sprawling climber. Its silvery, comb-shaped leaves go with almost anything, and it is ideal in a hot, sunny wall bed, where it will swarm up the wall and also tumble among the smaller plants below. *Helichrysum petiolare*, familiar as a bedding plant with heart-shaped, silvery-felted leaves, also behaves like a climber if encouraged. You might give it as a companion, one of the climbing alstroemerias, known as *Bomarea*, which also appreciate warm sheltered conditions. Some have clusters of clear bright orange flowers. Something less rare and tricky would be one of the new hybrid Cape figworts, *Phygelius* × *erectus*: 'Devil's Tears' is a dusky orange-pink that looks well with silver foliage.

Climbers need not grow upwards only. Here a sweep of golden-leaved heather forms the backdrop for Clematis 'Abundance'. In winter the clematis stems are cut almost to the ground to leave the stage clear for the heather to flower. Low conifers make equally suitable hosts: try a deep velvety red clematis such as 'Royal Velours' over Juniperus 'Grey Owl'.

CLIMBERS IN TREES

If, or when, you have a tree in your garden sufficiently mature to host a climber, you will find there is just as much scope for planning bright or subtle combinations as with shrubs.

Let us say you have moved into a house with some sort of garden, but nothing very inspiring. There is a tree, perhaps two, that seem rather dull. Before you rush to cut them down and plant something more exciting, stop to ask yourself a few questions. Is the tree hiding something you would rather not have to look at every day? Is it providing welcome shade in summer? Would it be a problem to get rid of? (Cutting down and removing a tree, including the stump and roots, is always more or less of a major job.) Could it not be given a new lease of life if you set a climber through its branches? The only trees that are unsuitable are the densely leafy ones such as sycamore, that would stifle a climber. The best candidates, apart from those that are performing some essential task like hiding an eyesore or filtering the wind, are the decorative trees with only one short season of effect. Rare trees are best left uncluttered.

A common hawthorn in a country garden could host one of the less vigorous synstylae roses, an orange peel clematis, or even a honeysuckle — if you accept the risk that the climber may choke the host to death in time. An old cherry in a town garden could be cheered up with a variegated ivy. A superannuated apple or pear tree would be well matched with one of the more domesticated rambler roses with double flowers. A plain green thuya or cypress would be transformed by a cascade of white *Clematis montana* in spring.

Again, matching vigour is important, perhaps even more important than with shrubs, because everything is on a larger scale, and correspondingly more difficult to put right. I wonder how many Kiftsgate roses there are that have become the despair of their owners, who forgot, or never knew, that the original Kiftsgate rose they admired fills three sizeable trees: not modest garden specimens, but full-sized forest trees.

You would need a large tree, too, for a wisteria, and a sizeable one for the Russian vine, *Polygonum baldschuanicum*, or for the climbing bittersweet, *Celastrus orbiculatus*. In warm climates like that of the Mediterranean you could grow the Banksian rose or *Bignonia capreolata* in a tall tree also.

Provided you bear in mind that question of comparative vigour, a tree could well hold not just one but two climbers, to extend the season still further. Suppose

Climbing perennial peas are ideal border plants. This unusual combination sets Lathyrus grandiflorus, *the everlasting pea, with* Cistus 'Silver Pink' *in a predominantly green setting that enhances the varied shades of pink. In a border of silvery foliage the pink of the pea and cistus would take on a different value.*

you decide on *Clematis montana* 'Grandiflora', setting its pure white blossom against a dark background. It could be paired with the rambler rose 'Francis E. Lester', for a succession of white, fragrant flowers in summer. You could do the same exercise in pink: *Clematis montana* 'Rubens' followed by rambler rose 'Paul's Himalayan Musk'. If you think a change of colour would be more fun, blue *Clematis macropetala* could be succeeded by rose 'Goldfinch'; or, the succession might be, not spring into summer as with these, but summer into autumn: a rambler rose first, then *Clematis tangutica* for flowers and silky seedheads.

Autumn foliage is often at its most beautiful when the sun shines through, not on, the scarlet or crimson or gold of the dying leaves. When you grow autumn-colouring climbers on a wall, you lose this incandescent effect, but not when they grow naturally through the branches of a tree. Try *Vitis coignetiae*, with its big leaves like dinner plates, through a silver birch, for the contrast not just of colour but also of leaf size; birches shed leaves like golden coins in autumn. The common Virginia creeper and Boston ivy are transformed too when grown like this.

Many climbers look finer when cascading from a height, and because their natural habit is to reach for the light, it should not be long before they make their way through the host tree and emerge in curtains of bloom. White rambler roses, the autumn-fruiting *Celastrus orbiculatus*, frothy *Clematis flammula*, these and others can be encouraged to grow in this way.

Trees with handsome trunks or beautiful bark should not be concealed by a self-clinging climber, but a tree with nothing special to offer in this department could well host a climbing hydrangea or one of the selected ivies or *Euonymus fortunei* varieties. The ivies and euonymus are especially good for adding winter interest to a deciduous tree of not especially distinguished outline, and golden variegations bring an impression of sunshine to the gloomy winter scene. Some people are nervous about ivy in trees, but ivy does not feed off the tree, merely uses it as a support. It will do no harm to a healthy tree, and may keep an ancient and hollow one upright. Only if the outer branches of the tree become too full of weighty ivy foliage will there be trouble. Keep the ivy to the trunk and main branches and all should be well.

Even a dead tree can support a climber. Although it is usually wise to remove dead trees completely, for reasons of garden hygiene, sometimes it is near impossible. And sometimes the trunk and main branches of the tree are so pictur-esque that to remove the carcase would seem sacrilegious. Instead, it can take on a new, vicarious life with a climber of medium vigour, or for a shorter stump a sprawling climber such as *Clematis × jouiniana*.

A choice few climbers need cool but sheltered conditions to evoke their native temperate rain forests. A mossy tree trunk is the ideal support for the Chilean *Asteranthera ovata*, a rare and almost hardy relative of the streptocarpus. Less uncommon, but still not a plant you see every day, its compatriot *Mitraria coccinea* has vivid scarlet trumpets and will sprawl or scramble upwards, rather like ivy.

CLIMBERS IN CLIMBERS

A climber can well be paired with another climber. Sometimes a climber may act, not only as a visual foil, but also as a support, to another of less rigid growth.

Usually, though, the reason for such marriages is aesthetic rather than practical.

The classic combination is a climbing rose with a clematis. In formal settings, on house walls, on pergolas, choose large-flowered roses and large-flowered clematis. Neither has much to offer except flowers: but what flowers. The high pointed blooms of the rose contrast with the wide flat blooms of the clematis. Clematis bring a colour absent from roses, a range of blues; never as pure as gentian, but close to tender sky blue or deeper, richer shades from lavender to violet. Such opulence of flower distracts the eye from the shapelessness of the plants themselves.

The presence of the blues, as well as a range of pinks always more or less suffused with lilac, and of course the whites and the purples, means you can devise complementary, harmonious or contrasting colour groupings with roses and clematis. Blue-violet *C*. 'Lasurstern' makes a rich blend with a deep red rose such as 'Etoile de Hollande' or 'Guinée'. Cooler, blue-mauve *C*. 'Mrs Cholmondeley' would suit a pink rose such as 'Caroline Testout, Clg', or the still paler 'Madame Butterfly, Clg' or its blush parent 'Ophelia Clg'. Both these old roses have beautiful scrolled blooms and have outlasted and outclassed newer varieties.

If you prefer the complementary colours of near-blue and yellow, mix porcelain blue *C*. 'Lady Northcliffe' with a clear yellow rose, 'Golden Showers', perhaps. Or set *C*. 'Lord Nevill', a violet-blue clematis, with yolk-yellow *R*. 'Lawrence Johnston'. The warmer yellow, suffused with apricot, of the Noisette roses such as 'Gloire de Dijon', is flattered by a violet-blue clematis such as 'The President', which has a silvery reverse to the bloom.

The coral pink of roses such as the old Daily Mail rose, 'Madame Edouard Herriot', also looks well with blue clematis. Blue and white is a fresh, cool combination; try *Clematis* 'Perle d'Azur' with the good old climbing rose 'Madame Alfred Carrière'. The ultimate in refinement is white with white: a clematis such as 'Marie Boisselot' or 'Henryi' could replace 'Perle d'Azur', or the rose might be 'Paul's Lemon Pillar', with huge pointed blooms as pale as lemon sorbet.

Roses and clematis are not the end of it, if you want to mix your climbers. I have often extolled the planting, on a half-shaded wall of a house, of *Clematis macropetala* 'Markham's Pink' with *Akebia quinata*. This is a lusty climber with cupped, chocolate-maroon flowers in spring, just right with the muted dusky pink of the clematis. Another eye-catching combination is Boston ivy or Virginia creeper with a variegated, bold-leaved true ivy: brilliant in scarlet, primrose and green in autumn, and comely in winter when the ivy has the scene to itself.

An ivy of this kind could be paired with a climbing hydrangea instead, or the hydrangea could host *Tropaeolum speciosum*, so that its own white, lacecap flowers are followed by the bright scarlet of the flame flower.

The claret vine is the ideal companion for the dusty pink passion flower, *Passiflora × caerulea-racemosa*, on a sheltered wall in cool areas, or in warmer gardens on a gazebo or pergola. With enough space you could add to a group like this, with slate-blue *Solanum jasminoides*, claret and purple *Rhodochiton atrosanguineum*, a lilac-pink double clematis, one of the 'blue' rambler roses. By keeping to a fairly narrow range of colours you can be sure that nothing will clash. You could add some silvery foliage at the base of the wall, bed out heliotrope for fragrance in summer, and plant nerine bulbs for their bright candy pink, crimpled autumn flowers.

CLIMBERS ON HEDGES

Informal hedges, especially, lend themselves to hosting a climber. The hedge is, after all, no more than a line of close-planted shrubs, and we have seen how effective climbers and shrubs can be together. A climber can give the cosmetic treatment to a gappy hedge — try *Lonicera japonica*, a vigorous semi-evergreen honeysuckle. In country hedges you will often find a common honeysuckle growing. Trimmed hawthorn plus honeysuckle makes a cottagey hedge suitable for a country garden. Rambling roses also deck hedgerows in the country and could just as well do so in the garden.

If you have a formal hedge of clipped yew or cypress, then you need to use climbers with more restraint, if at all. The example to follow, often extolled, is the flame flower on the trim yew hedges of Hidcote Manor gardens in Gloucestershire, a place of pilgrimage for all devotees of English gardens. The herbaceous stems of the climber are so slender, its foliage so exiguous, that the hedge is unaffected. *Adlumia fungosa*, a frail-looking biennial fumitory with pink flowers, is another that would do no harm. *Eccremocarpus scaber*, though vigorous, is little leafy, and dies down, or indeed dies completely, in winter. The variegated hop has more generous foliage, but is grown as an annual.

The best sort of hedge to festoon with climbers, apart from the rough country hedgerow, is the one composed of flowering shrubs, not clipped to geometric neatness but allowed to grow with minimal interference, pruned rather than clipped. Pink *Escallonia* could host the climbing monkshood, a *Rosa rugosa* hedge would suit *Clematis viticella*, a tall hedge of sea buckthorn could cope with *C. orientalis*.

CLIMBERS IN MIXED BORDERS

Almost all these ways of growing climbers can be appropriate in mixed borders, where in little space they will give you scope for more fragrance, more colour, more flower, more foliage, more height, as you desire. Let me illustrate by picking out two combinations of climber plus host shrub, and building on the theme suggested.

Suppose you have a specimen of *Pyrus salicifolia*, the weeping silver pear, grown past lanky adolescence. A bold clematis, the velvety purple *C.* 'Gipsy Queen' or plum-purple 'Star of India' with its deep carmine bar on each tepal, stands out dramatically on the silvery dome of the pear. Allow a few strands of the clematis to stray onto *Rosa glauca* nearby, and further still into *Ceanothus* 'Gloire de Versailles' and the madder pink *Deutzia* 'Rosealind'. *Lavatera olbia* 'Rosea' or the palest blush, pink-eyed 'Barnsley', add a clearer pink note to enrich the clematis colouring. At the feet of these tallish shrubs could be grown the purple sage, *Salvia officinalis* 'Purpurascens'; nepeta for a bluer note; mauve-pink phloxes for peppery summer scent; *Aster thomsonii* in clear lavender-blue; *Geranium psilostemon* with

In an informal mixed border setting, the bold, toothed leaves of Helleborus corsicus, *its jade green flowers long over, make a grey-green plinth for the wide flowers of* Clematis *'Kathleen Wheeler' and the lacy pink of* Hydrangea serrata. *Clematis are extremely adaptable, and you certainly do not need a wall to grow them.*

flowers of magenta, wickedly black-eyed. The tall spears of *Verbena bonariensis* add a deeper note of violet-purple echoing the strong tones of the clematis. All that is for summer. You can imagine spring/autumn combinations to extend the season.

Maybe pinks and mauves are not your thing. You can build schemes with the sharper colours, and all the sunset shades, just as well. Let us say your principal shrub ingredients are *Philadelphus coronarius* 'Aureus' for its lime-yellow foliage, and *Rosa moyesii* 'Geranium' for its blood red flowers and vermilion hips. At their feet you have planted scarlet *Crocosmia* 'Lucifer', yellow daylilies, yellow potentillas or perhaps the tangerine 'Red Ace', and *Alchemilla mollis* for its lime green froth of flower and soft fan-shaped leaves. *Lonicera × brownii* 'Fuchsioides' in scarlet, and *Eccremocarpus scaber* in typical orange, or in selected amber or crimson strains, can run through the branches of your shrubs, and a stout pole be wreathed in the bold primrose and green leaves of *Hedera colchica* 'Sulphur Heart'.

4
THE
PRACTICALITIES

I HOPE THAT THE PRECEDING pages have fired you with enthusiasm to grow more climbers, in more imaginative ways. It is time to say a little about the practicalities.

PLANTING AND AFTERCARE

Growing climbers is much like growing any other plant. So common sense, and the treatment we give our other plants, will do very well. Plant bare-root climbers, if deciduous and hardy, during open weather in late autumn and winter unless you live where the winters are very cold, when everything will have to be planted in spring. The less hardy deciduous climbers, and evergreen ones, are better planted during early autumn or spring. Hardy container-grown climbers can be planted whenever the ground is neither frozen, waterlogged, nor parched.

Preparing the site

In the wild, climbers normally grow at woodland edges or among low shrubs, and are therefore happiest with cool roots in humus-rich soil. The best humus is the kind that also feeds: well-rotted garden compost, farmyard or stable manure, leaf-mould, bracken mould. Peat, and substitutes with similar qualities such as ground bark or coco fibre, should be regarded as simple humus without much nutrient content.

Walls and fences often keep much of the rain away, and hedges are greedy. This means the soil becomes dry and impoverished, so you should take extra care if you are planting in these conditions, or your climbers may suffer as a result. The soil at the foot of a wall may also be very poor; the topsoil may have been carted away by the builders, leaving you with only subsoil.

Remember that you are likely to be asking a good deal of your climbers. The abundance of bloom you will hope for makes heavy demands on the plants, which must be able to replenish themselves through their roots.

Planting

Soak the roots of your climbers thoroughly before you plant them. In dry weather it is often worth puddling in. Pour a full bucket of water into the planting hole — which should, of course, be large enough to accommodate the climber's roots without cramping them — just before planting. Make sure that the roots are carefully teased out and soil sifted among them and gently firmed, following up with more water once the soil is firmed around the roots.

Most climbers should be planted at the same depth as they were growing before. An exception is clematis, which will benefit from deeper planting, so that there is a pair of buds below the soil surface to act as reserve if the topgrowth is stricken by wilt.

Planting climbers to grow into trees

Climbers to decorate a host tree also need extra careful preparation, because they will have to compete with the root system of the tree.

You may be able to find a gap between the main anchoring roots of the tree, quite close to the trunk. This works reasonably well, especially with mature, deep-rooted trees that do not make a dense mat of feeding roots. But the soil is likely to be very dry, so you will need to water in very thoroughly, give an annual mulch at a time when the soil is still moist, and ideally also scatter a slow-release fertilizer each year.

If you cannot find a gap among the roots near the tree, then you will have to go outside the area of the feeding roots, and lead the climber into the outer branches of the canopy.

It is often helpful to give the climber a head start by the box technique. Dig your planting hole as usual, at least 1 m (3 ft) square if possible, and line it with a bottomless box made of thin, decayable boards. Fill with the prepared soil mixture and plant in the usual way. The wood will rot fairly quickly, but the year or two it takes will give the climber time to establish before the tree roots invade its station.

Aftercare

After planting, mulch your climber with more humus, to keep its roots cool and retain moisture. For mulching, ground bark or coco fibre do very well. All climbers will benefit from an annual feed with general purpose fertilizer, plus a fresh mulch on moist soil.

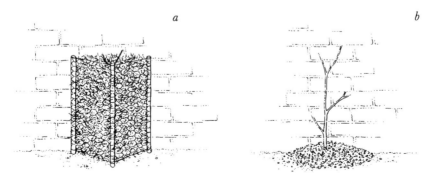

Fig. 10. Winter protection of tender climbers against a wall, (a) a 'cage' of chicken wire stuffed with bracken, straw or dry leaves; (b) a heap of grit over the roots.

You may also need to protect your climbers against frost and wind, especially when newly planted or if they are a little tender. Wind has a drying effect; while freezing winds both chill and desiccate. You can protect climbers with bracken, conifer branches, proprietary windscreening, or purpose-made screens of chicken wire sandwiching bracken or straw (Fig. 10*a*). If you use plastic of any kind, do not enclose the plant completely except in emergencies of extreme weather, or it will be unable to breathe and moulds may form, with dire results. In winters that are both cold and wet a plastic jacket, held away from the plant with canes, and stuffed during very cold spells with insulating bracken or straw, may be needed. Some climbers, such as *Passiflora caerulea*, are able to regenerate from the roots if their topgrowth is frosted, so a heap of grit or ashes about the roots and main stem may be protection enough (Fig. 10*b*).

HOW THEY CLIMB

To train your climber effectively, it is helpful to know how climbers attach themselves, so that you can work with the plant, not against it.

Many climbing plants hoist themselves upwards by *twining* their stems around the host's branches. Familiar climbers like wisteria, honeysuckle (Fig. 11), scarlet runner bean, and — among weeds — bindweed, have twining stems, woody or herbaceous.

Ivy, on the other hand, is one of the climbers that attach themselves by *aerial* roots, which can be extremely tenacious (Fig. 12). They are not feeding roots, but are adapted purely for sticking to their supports.

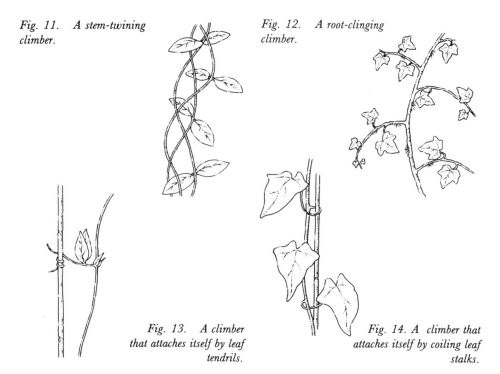

Fig. 11.   A stem-twining climber.

Fig. 12.   A root-clinging climber.

Fig. 13.   A climber that attaches itself by leaf tendrils.

Fig. 14. A climber that attaches itself by coiling leaf stalks.

Several climbers cling by *tendrils* derived from the leaf (Fig. 13) or from the stipules, or by coiling leaf stalks (Fig. 14). The last is the way of clematis. Sweet peas are tendril climbers, and so is *Cobaea scandens*; *Macfadyena unguis-cati*, the cat's claw vine, has tendrils equipped with little hooks. The leaf tendrils of some members of the genus *Parthenocissus*, in the vine family, have little adhesive pads at the tips, so the plants self-stick as efficiently as a climber with aerial roots.

The least tenacious of climbers are those that simply haul themselves up by means of *hooks*, or by pushing their scrambling stems through neighbouring plants. The hooks or prickles can be on the stems, as in roses, or on the backs of the leaves or at the leaf tips, as in *Gloriosa superba*.

METHODS OF SUPPORT

Only self-sticking climbers with aerial roots or adhesive tendrils will be able to climb a wall, fence or pole without help. Even then you may need to assist the plant a little in the first years. Every other climber will need artificial supports of some kind.

Climbers on walls and fences

One of the most satisfactory supports on a wall, not expensive to instal and very unobtrusive once the climbers have grown, is to set vine eyes into the wall. They should be long enough to leave 10 cm (4 in) or so clear of the wall after insertion, and are then linked by braided wire (which does not sag like plain galvanized wire) running both horizontally and vertically, so you end up with a widely spaced mesh of wire over the wall's surface. If possible, use tensioning bolts with the wire to ensure it is tautly stretched.

Nails are a poor substitute for vine eyes, though you can often find a specially shaped nail, a long, tapering triangle with a hole for the wire in the broad end. These are cheap to buy.

An alternative to wires is a trellis of some kind. The most effective, a well-built wooden trellis, is expensive unless you are handy enough to make your own. The kind of trellis that you buy ready made, folded concertina fashion, and pull out to fill the space you have available, is cheaper, and looks it. Whether ready made or custom built, trellis panels should be treated with a non-toxic wood preservative, preferably colourless. After treatment, the trellis should be fixed at about 10 cm (4 in) from the wall.

Plastic-covered trellis or mesh can be bought in white, green or brown. Fix it onto a strong frame, so that you can leave a space between it and the wall. This space gives the climber room to get behind the supports the better to attach itself, and allows air to move freely between the wall and the climber. All except self-stickers are the better for fresh air through their stems.

Many fences, such as chain link or chestnut paling, are so constructed that they offer a fair substitute for natural supports, but solid fences such as larch lap will need to be treated more like a wall. Wires could be stretched between the uprights, to which you have fixed vine eyes. On a post and rail or ranch-style fence the occasional discreet support, say a strategically placed staple to which you can attach a plant tie, should be enough.

Climbers on pergolas and arches

On pergolas and arches you will most likely choose twining climbers for the cross-beams. They may need support at first, before they reach the top of the pillars. Once they have gained the crossbeams, their own twining stems will hold them firmly enough in most circumstances. The stiffer or shorter growing climbers you plant against the uprights may need tying in each year.

Much the same goes for poles or tripods. Some people wrap a pole that is to hold a climber in plastic mesh. Do it if you must; but it will look awful until the climber completely covers it, and awful again in winter if you have chosen a deciduous climber. Better to spend a little time each season tying the stems to the pole with soft garden string. A tie about every 15 cm (6 in) will be right. A self-clinger such as ivy will of course need no tying-in once it has taken hold.

Climbers in trees

Climbers in trees also need help in the early stages to reach branches small enough to twine or coil around. If you have planted your climber outside the area of the feeding roots, you could use a cane to lead it to the branches, or run a stout rope from the branch to a stake driven in by the climber. If you plant to windward, gales will blow it more firmly into the arms of the host instead of tearing it away from its support. If you find straying stems — roses are especially prone to this — guide them back into the branches using a long, forked stick. Once they have reached high enough, stems that grow out and down are to be encouraged. One of the great sights of summer is a falling cascade of white rambler rose in a dark-leaved host tree.

PRUNING

Many people, especially when quite new to gardening, seem unaccountably scared of pruning. Yet pruning is neither an abstruse and difficult art, nor an exact and demanding science. Mostly, it is a matter of common sense.

Its purpose is to keep the plant looking its best; to encourage it to form a sound and shapely framework of branches; to promote an abundant and well-displayed crop of flowers or fruit or both; to remove dead or diseased growth; to keep the plant within bounds if it grows with too much exuberance.

It is easy to show just how subjective a matter pruning is if you read the instructions of half a dozen different writers on how to prune a newly-planted climber. Some will say that you should prune lightly until the main framework of branches has grown to fill the allotted space. Others maintain that you should prune quite hard in spring following planting, to encourage stout growth and branching from low down. My own inclination is to leave alone, or prune only lightly, if the plant is healthy, well branched and well rooted; but to remove any spindly stems or cut them back to a plump bud in the hope of encouraging new, lustier growth.

There is also the question of annual pruning; do you or don't you, and if you do, when? The rule of thumb is quite simple. Plants that flower on the current year's growths — generally, the ones that flower after mid summer — need to be pruned in late winter or early spring. This will give them the longest possible growing period to form new shoots to bear the next crop of flowers.

Plants that flower on last year's stems, that is those that flower early in the year and not later than mid summer, should be pruned immediately after they have flowered. The growths that then form will bear next year's flowers. Of course, if you expect a crop of fruits to follow the flowers, this is not the way to prune, for you will be cutting away the forming fruits.

To prune or not to prune?

Very often the choice is yours between regular pruning or virtually no pruning. This is true of many clematis, for example the popular *Clematis montana*. If you prune it each year after flowering, it will take up less room, and give you a display of flowers that will each be larger than on an unpruned plant. If you want a great cascade of bloom, then leave it alone. Then, of course, the time may come when it has become too big, or cluttered with dead growths. If you cut right back into the old wood of the main stem at this stage, you run the risk that it may not re-generate. On the other hand, it may. And if it does not, well, you have space to plant something else, even if it is only a better variety of *Clematis montana* than the one you have just killed.

You need, often, to exercise a little foresight. Is the climber likely to become too large for the space if you do not prune it? Then it is better to prune regularly than to leave things alone until you have an unsightly tangle which you then hack back in desperation.

Despite the rule of thumb about when to prune, I am inclined to think that there is never a wrong time to remove thin and weak or diseased shoots — except when it is so cold that the cut ends of the stems would get frosted. Always, whatever kind of pruning you are doing, use a good quality pair of secateurs, and keep them sharp and in good order. Snags and tears are unsightly, and disease enters more easily through damaged tissues than through a clean cut.

The one kind of 'pruning' to avoid at all costs is the 'parks and gardens haircut' style, when all the stems are clipped back as though the poor plant was part of a hedge. Pruning properly consists of cutting out all or part of whole stems, one at a time, considering as you go the appearance of the plant and how each cut will affect the future growth. Once you bring common sense and intelligence to bear on the problem in this way, it ceases to be a problem at all and becomes one of the more enjoyable and creative aspects of gardening. You are brought into intimate contact with your plants, getting to know them as individuals; and the work is not by any means physically demanding, unless you have no head for heights.

PESTS AND DISEASES

Climbers are generally remarkably free of pests and diseases. If you treat them well, and ensure that you remove dead growths, fallen leaves and spent flowers scrupulously, you should have little trouble. A strongly growing plant is more resistant to pests and diseases than a weakling; and an uncluttered one offers less shelter for pests to lurk in. But for all that, you cannot expect to escape entirely unscathed.

Pests

Aphids, which are sap-sucking insects, are one of the most common pests. Climbers infested with **greenfly** or **blackfly** show the usual symptoms of stunted or deformed growth, with fewer flowers than normal. Honeysuckles are especially susceptible. The aphids also exude honeydew, a delightful name for a substance which results in horrid black sooty moulds on the leaves. Aphids are also often responsible for spreading virus diseases. It is thus worth taking prompt action. If you are willing to use chemicals, spray with a proprietary insecticide, or use a systemic. Systemic pesticides are especially useful for plants like honeysuckle where the aphids are so hidden between the clasping pairs of leaves that killing them with a spray is almost impossible. 'Green' gardeners will choose the least harmful pesticides, especially those made from natural materials; or simply blast the aphids off the plants with a strong jet of water.

    Capsid bugs are sap-suckers that kill the plant tissue where they feed, giving the characteristic tattered, holey appearance of affected leaves. Again, a treatment with insecticide may be necessary; so, too, for certain leaf-eating pests, including **caterpillars** (which can be picked off individually if not too numerous), **earwigs** and **leafminers**. These last actually live inside the leaf, eating the soft tissues between the upper and lower surfaces and leaving the characteristic pale trace as they tunnel their way along. Honeysuckles, again, are rather susceptible. Earwigs can be killed by more old fashioned methods. Fill a flowerpot with straw, upend it on a cane and leave it among affected plants. Each morning, especially while the evenings are warm, empty the flowerpot of its earwigs and destroy them.

    The rose has its own particular leaf pest: the **leaf rolling rose sawfly**, which rolls the leaves up tightly. Pick off and destroy affected leaves, or if there is a serious infestation, use a systemic insecticide.

    Stems may be affected by pests too: **scale insects** and **froghoppers**. The froghopper larva, a small green creature, creates as a protection for its soft body the frothy masses known as cuckoospit. If they are not too many, they can be squashed singly.

    Slugs are a threat mainly to tender young growths. They are most active when the weather is damp. There are several different types of slug control now available, including 'green' methods, or you can simply drop kitchen salt on each slug you see, or put out a slug bar. This is a saucer filled with beer; slugs seem to like the stuff, and you may find your saucer filled each morning with a slimy mixture of beer and dead slugs. For the wholly non-squeamish, stamping on them with a heavy boot disposes of slugs very effectively. Clematis shoots are a particular delicacy for slugs; especially the tender new shoots that arise after a large-flowered clematis has been stricken by wilt and you are nursing it back to health. Special vigilance is needed. Damage at soil level which is not caused by slugs is often the work of **cutworms**, which can be kept at bay by insecticidal dust.

    Under glass, the chief pests are **red spider mite** and **whitefly**. Red spider mite are sap suckers, so tiny that they are usually detected only by the symptoms they cause, of mottled and discoloured leaves; though sometimes they give themselves away by weaving a fine, silken web. They love the warm, dry conditions of a glasshouse, so you may be able to control them simply by increasing the humidity. A bad attack may need chemical control. Whitefly are like tiny pale moths, and in a bad infestation they rise like a stifling cloud whenever your plants are disturbed. They damage plants in much the same way as aphids, excreting honeydew which encourages the growth of sooty mould.

Some people have had good results with biological control of glasshouse pests, especially on commercial crops. Whitefly can be controlled by introducing the tiny wasp *Encarsia formosa*, which is parasitic on whitefly larvae. At low temperatures the whitefly breeds faster than the wasp, but at higher temperatures (from 18°C [64°F], most effectively at over 24°C [73°F]) the wasp increases faster. Good light levels are also necessary for control. Introduce the parasite at fortnightly intervals, starting as soon as you see the first whitefly in spring.

Red spider mite can be destroyed by its predator *Phytoseiulus persimilis*. You need to order 30 to 50 of the predator per infested plant. Unlike the encarsia wasp, these do better at temperatures below 24°C (73°F). After two weeks, they should start reducing the mite population and may eliminate it altogether.

Diseases

Many of the common diseases of plants are caused by fungus of one kind or another. In wet seasons **botrytis** is often a problem. Leaves and stems that are affected are covered with a furry grey fungal growth. The fungus often first infects dead tissue and then spreads to the living parts of the plant: always pick off and remove dead leaves.

Powdery mildew, on the other hand, is worse in dry, still conditions. It shows as a powdery white film on leaves, buds and stems. Many rambler roses are very susceptible to mildew, and those that are should never be grown against a wall, but always in the open where the air can blow freely through their stems. Both these fungal diseases can be controlled by spraying with a suitable fungicide. Commercial growers often use more than one, in rotation, to avoid the build up of resistance to a particular chemical.

Silverleaf is a disease most familiar in plums; it can also affect honeysuckles. The treatment consists of cutting back all the affected parts to healthy tissue.

Roses, especially the more highly bred ones, have their own fungal problems, notably **black spot** and **rust**. Here more than ever hygiene is important. Always remove all fallen leaves at the season's end, and of course any that are affected by the characteristic black spots, or rust-coloured freckles most noticeable on the reverse of the leaves, during the growing season. Burn them; on no account attempt to compost them. Rust is the harder to control, and very badly affected plants should be dug up and burnt. Milder attacks, and most infections of black spot, can be treated with a suitable fungicide.

The corresponding blight of clematis is **wilt**. It affects especially the large-flowered cultivars, which can seem perfectly healthy one day and succumb the next. Sometimes only a few shoots are affected, sometimes the whole plant collapses. Remove all affected parts, and spray whatever is left, and the sur-rounding soil, with benomyl at regular intervals. And remember the warning about slugs and the new growths that you hope will form from below ground.

Few mature gardens are entirely free of **honey fungus**, which can affect woody climbers. If a plant suddenly wilts and dies for no apparent reason, suspect honey fungus. When you lift the corpse, you may find the characteristic black 'bootlaces', correctly called rhizomorphs, of the fungus. There are various pro-prietary products said to control honey fungus; some people say they are effective, others not. Good cultivation is probably the best defence; a stressed plant is much more likely to succumb if the fungus is present in the soil.

Virus disease is a portmanteau description of other troubles that affect plants. Infected specimens are usually stunted, and the leaves are often discoloured or distorted. The only cure is to dig out and burn the whole plant.

PROPAGATION

Though it may sometimes be necessary to destroy a plant that is diseased, it is much pleasanter to spend time making new plants. For this reason, in the chapters that follow, I shall mention propagation for virtually all the plants I describe. In this chapter I shall describe, briefly, methods that anyone can use who has space enough to put a pot or two on a windowsill, a garden frame, a home propagating unit. Large-scale commercial growers often make use of techniques that are inappropriate for the amateur. But even the professionals also use methods that are almost identical, except in scale, to what we do in our small, private gardens.

Cuttings

Cuttings are the chief method used to propagate garden varieties which we want to keep true to type. Stem cuttings are of two kinds: dormant, or green and leafy. Each needs different treatment.

Dormant cuttings or **hardwood cuttings** are taken in autumn or early winter, from ripe shoots of the season. Cut them cleanly beneath a node (leaf joint), and remove the tips just above a node, to make cuttings about 20–30 cm (8–12 in) long. Insert the cuttings to two thirds their length in a narrow V-shaped trench in sandy soil, firm the soil around them, and water them in. After a year they should be well rooted and ready to lift.

Green cuttings are of two kinds: **soft cuttings** (Fig. 15a), taken from young shoots that have not yet hardened up; and **half-ripe** (Fig. 15b) or **semi-hardwood** cuttings taken later in the season, when they are firm at the base but still quite soft at the tips.

Both kinds can be renewed from the mother plant with a heel of harder wood at the base, or cut just below a node. The heel should be neatly trimmed so that it is hardly more than a swelling at the base of the cutting. Less often they are cut between two leaf joints, when they are called **internodal cuttings**. Clematis and honeysuckles are often treated in this way. Remove the lower leaves of the cutting carefully with a sharp knife or razor blade. If the remaining leaves are large or thin-textured, you can reduce them in size: compound leaves have one or more

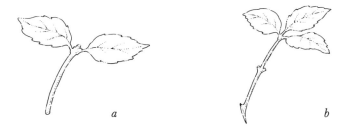

Fig. 15.   A soft cutting (a) *and a semi-ripe cutting with a heel* (b).

leaflets removed, simple leaves are neatly sliced through. This helps to reduce water loss through transpiration while the cutting has no roots to sustain it.

The cutting compost may be half peat and half sand, or you may mix in perlite or coarse grit. Whether you use hormone rooting powders or solutions is largely up to you. I suspect that most soft cuttings would root perfectly well without hormones, but that the fungicide incorporated in the powder or liquid may help to keep the cuttings from rotting while they form roots.

The chief threat to cuttings is moulds, particularly botrytis, so it is always well to water them in with a fungicidal solution. Once a week while the cuttings are still in a close atmosphere, spray or water again with fungicide. If you can alternate two or even three different chemicals, so much the better.

The cuttings once struck and watered in, must be kept in a close, humid atmosphere until they have formed roots. This can be achieved by covering the cuttings with very fine plastic film (the kind used in kitchens, called clingfilm) or making a tent of a heavier grade of clear plastic over them. A propagating case achieves the same effect but more expensively.

Propagating cases are useful for cuttings that need bottom heat. Some slightly tricky plants will root much more readily if the cuttings have this extra stimulus. You can also provide bottom heat by laying cables in a cold frame. The same frame could be used to overwinter young plants that are slightly tender.

If you are using the simpler and cheaper method of covering the cuttings with plastic, turn the film frequently to avoid a build-up of condensation. Keep a specially close watch on cuttings with downy or felty foliage, where trapped moisture forms an ideal breeding ground for moulds. As soon as new shoots start to form, indicating that there is root growth below, start gradually to let air in to wean the cuttings. Once the cuttings are well rooted, they can be potted on individually.

A very simple method for easy climbers and other woody plants is to take half-ripe cuttings in summer and set them in sandy, open soil in the ground, covering them with a long plastic cloche. Most honeysuckles, for example, respond very well to this treatment. Because they are in the ground, the roots can search for nourishment, and you quickly get a plump young plant that is unlikely to suffer a check unless you forget to water the cuttings regularly. To avoid scorch, you can use semi-opaque white plastic, or cover clear plastic with green, woven shading material, easy to remove on dull days.

Some specialized cuttings

1. *Clematis.* Take cuttings from about mid summer, cutting between the nodes. You will end up with a pair of buds and leaves, and about 5 cm (2 in) of stem (Fig. 16). Remove one leaf, and reduce the size of the other if it is very large. It is helpful to use a hormone rooting compound and to water the cuttings in with a solution of fungicide, which you will also use from time to time when damping over. The biggest threat to clematis cuttings is grey mould.

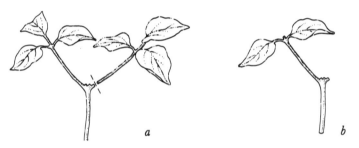

Fig. 16. Preparing clematis cuttings; (a) the internodal cutting showing where cuts are to be made; (b) the prepared cutting with one whole leaf and the terminal leaflet of the other removed.

Keep the cuttings shaded at first, and gradually give them more light once shoots form, probably in about four or five weeks. Reduce the watering gradually also. By autumn the roots should be well formed. Leave the cuttings in their pot and remove all the dead leaves. In early spring the rooted cuttings can be individually potted and staked, to grow on until summer when they can be planted out. Easy clematis to root in this way are the montanas and the atragenes. If you doubt your abilities, try these first and gain confidence.

2. *Vines.* A type of cutting used for vines in the genus *Vitis* is the **single bud cutting** (Fig. 17) Choose mature stems, and select well-formed buds, which you can cut with about 2 cm (just under 1 in) of stem on either side. Remove a sliver of stem from the side opposite the bud. You then simply press the cut surface horizontally into a pot filled with cutting compost, and place it in a heated propagator. Clematis can also be propagated in this way.

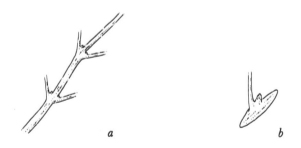

Fig. 17. A single bud cutting (b) cut from a stem of vine (a).

3. *Root cuttings.* Some climbers, such as *Campsis* among woody plants and *Tropaeolum speciosum* among herbaceous, can be increased in this way. You take sections of root about 3 cm (1½ in) long and insert them in a pot of cutting compost, vertically if they are stout enough, horizontally if they are very fine. The best time to take root cuttings is during the dormant season.

After a while, new shoots will grow from the top of the root cutting, followed by new root growth. The young plants can be potted individually, or lined out in a nursery plot to grow on.

Seed

If taking cuttings is the most unnatural way to make more of your climbers, sowing seed is the closest to nature's way. All annual and biennial climbers are grown from seed, as well as many fast-growing but tender perennials which will flower in their first year from seed. Longer-lived climbers will take correspondingly longer to reach a stage of maturity at which they will flower. Pure species, especially if not growing near others that are closely related, should come reasonably or entirely 'true'; hybrids will not.

Sow seed of climbers just as you sow other seeds, using for preference a proprietary compost, which will have been sterilized. Annuals will almost always come up very quickly, but some seeds, especially the ones with a fleshy covering, may need a period of dormancy before they will germinate. Alternating heat and cold, as well as moisture, may be needed to break dormancy. This applies more to woody plants and especially to those from areas where the winters are cold.

The simplest way of breaking the dormancy of such seeds is to emulate nature, by sowing seeds in autumn and leaving them outside to undergo the normal winter fluctuations in temperature. Be sure to protect the seeds against vermin. Many will then duly germinate in spring. It is wise, almost always, to rub off the flesh of fruits before sowing the seed.

Another technique is to stratify the seeds. Mix them with moist sand and set them in layers between more sand in a pot or perforated container. They are then either set outside to get frosted and thawed, or given spells of artificial cold and warm weather with the assistance of a refrigerator and a glasshouse. By late winter the seeds are ready to sow, and should germinate promptly in the spring.

Layering

Some climbers layer themselves easily and naturally in the wild. With their usually supple stems, climbers are often easier to increase in this way than other woody plants. It is a method that is useful both for some easy-rooting plants, such as *Rubus*, and for those than can be obdurate about making roots from cuttings, such as *Vitis coignetiae*.

Choose shoots that are near ground level or can be bent down to reach it, and that are neither too soft and young nor too old and woody. Having made a short, angled cut in the underside of the stem, about 30 cm (1 ft) from the tip, and dusted the cut with hormone rooting powder, you peg the shoot down to the ground (Fig. 18). Gently bend the tip of the chosen stem towards the vertical and tie it to a cane.

Fig. 18.   Layering climbers: a suitable shoot pegged into prepared soil and tied to a cane.

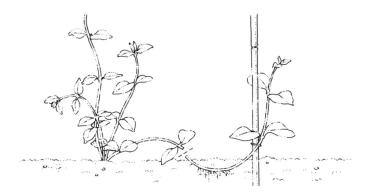

Fig. 19.   The rooted layer, severed but not yet lifted.

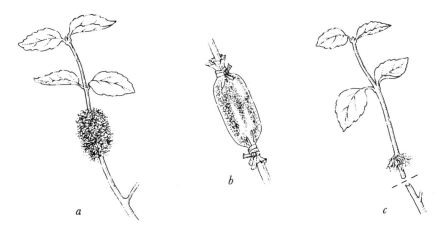

Fig. 20.   Air-layering: (a) surrounding the stem with sphagnum moss; (b) the stem and moss are kept moist with a sleeve of plastic; (c) the rooted layer is cut away from the stock plant.

When new roots are well formed, cut the layer away from the stock plant (Fig. 19).

Air-layering is a variant on the theme, used when there are no convenient stems that can reach ground level. The method is basically the same, except that you use moist sphagnum moss in place of soil (Fig. 20). Wrap it firmly around the cut section of the chosen stem, tie it in place with raffia or soft string, and wrap it in plastic to keep the moisture in. Once roots have formed, sever the stem from the parent and pot it up.

Other ways to make more plants

Herbaceous border plants are commonly increased by division of the rootstock. Some climbers, especially herbaceous ones, can be multiplied in the same way. Some climbers form suckers, which can be detached complete with their roots. The best time for either of these operations is late winter or early spring.

Whatever anyone, myself included, may say about 'the best time', never be put off if someone offers you a cutting or a sucker or a division at the 'wrong' time. Very often, the best time to perform any operation — propagation, planting, pruning — is when you are in the mood. Plants are often tougher and more willing to grow than we give them credit for. If the only time you are likely to be offered that coveted cutting or sucker is mid winter or the middle of a heat wave, take it. It may well grow; but if you don't take it, it certainly will not.

5
THE QUEEN OF CLIMBERS

CLIMBING ROSES, LIKE THEIR shrubby cousins, come in many guises. From the original wild species have been developed rambler roses with single or double flowers, pillar roses and climbers with hybrid-tea blooms. These large-flowered kinds are perhaps what most people first think of as 'climbing roses'. Climbing roses are usually propagated commercially by budding. However, on a small scale, cuttings are often very successful: semi-ripe summer cuttings, or hardwood cuttings in autumn.

LARGE-FLOWERED CLIMBING ROSES

Many of the climbing roses with hybrid-tea blooms arose as sports of bush roses. There are of course far fewer of them than of the bush roses, and that may partly explain why several very old varieties are still cherished while bush roses come and go in just a few years. Another reason may be that on a bush rose a nodding flower is unwelcome, while on a climber it is elegant and graceful, and allows us to look into the heart of the flower from below. Not all the large-flowered climbing roses are sports from bush roses, however. The lovely 'New Dawn', for example, is a sport from a once-flowering rambler. Several are of mixed parentage. There are also what are loosely known as modern climbers, with large blooms of varying shapes, single, semi-double, or full-petalled, often of rather short growth which makes them very suitable for pillars, as well as walls.

Roses of this type are generally pruned in late winter, when thin and twiggy growths are removed, and flowering side shoots are cut back to two to four buds. As the plants age, it may be necessary to cut out a very old stem right at the base, from time to time; promising young growths forming near the base should be encouraged as potential replacements.

Red roses, symbol of love

Most people love a red rose, and to have soul, a red rose should also be fragrant. Some of the old climbers are still unequalled for perfume, such as 'Château de

Opposite: *The blooms of* Rosa *'Madame Grégoire Staechelin' come in one great burst at mid summer, transforming these pillars and their linking ropes into a swag of opulent blossom. Many roses with supple stems can be grown in this way.*

Clos Vougeot, Clg'. It has a sumptuous fragrance from velvety deep red blooms with repeat season, and grows to 4.5 m (15 ft). Two of the most famous and most fragrant must be 'Etoile de Hollande, Clg'. with deep crimson blooms; and 'Guinée' in deep maroon red, the shapely, richly fragrant blooms borne on growth of 3 m (10 ft). Both have a repeat season. So does 'Souvenir de Claudius Denoyel', a fine old rose of taller growth, with elegant, deep scarlet-red, intensely fragrant blooms.

Then there are two slightly newer perfumed red roses, 'Ena Harkness, Clg', with deep red, nodding blooms, once-flowering, growing to 4.5 m (15 ft); and 'Crimson Glory, Clg', its deep crimson blooms fading towards purple. It has a repeat season and grows to 4.5 m (15 ft).

'Paul's Scarlet Climber' is a red of a different style, bright crimson-scarlet, with loose blooms and a slight fragrance. It too is recurrent, and grows to 6 m (20 ft). 'Allen Chandler' is a nearly single, bright crimson-red rose, flowering twice a season if well fed, when it should reach 4.5 m (15 ft).

If you prefer your red roses to lean towards scarlet and orange, try 'Réveil Dijonnais', a scarlet and yellow semi-double bicolor, with some fragrance, a repeat season, and good foliage, growing up to 3 m (10 ft); or 'Danse du Feu', its bright orange-red, loose petalled flowers borne over a long season. It grows to 4 m (13 ft). In a class of its own for colour is 'Super Star, Clg', a short grower up to 2.5 m (8 ft) with striking vermilion HT blooms.

Pink roses to enchant

Red roses are the stuff of romance, but a pink rose always charms. For fragrance it is hard to beat 'Aloha', a pillar rose of 2.5 m (8 ft) or so with full-petalled pink blooms over a long season, and good dark foliage. The lovely old 'Ophelia, Clg', has high-pointed blush pink blooms, very fragrant, and recurrent. She gave rise to two sports with the same elegant blooms, good foliage, and growth of 4 m (13 ft) or so: 'Madame Butterfly, Clg', with pink to blush, scrolled, fragrant blooms, and 'Lady Sylvia, Clg' in rich pink.

'Madame Caroline Testout' is a famous old rose with satin pink, full-petalled flowers, slightly fragrant, and an autumn repeat. It grows to 4.5 m (15 ft). Another of similar dimensions is 'Madame Grégoire Staechelin', which has one great burst of huge pale pink, fragrant HT blooms with deeper reverse. The ever-popular 'New Dawn' is really a repeat-flowering rambler, but its pointed buds, opening to shell pink fragrant blooms in clusters, are very like a small HT's flowers. It reaches 3 m (10 ft).

'Pink Perpétué' is a fine modern climber or pillar rose, with clusters of scented, deep pink blooms over a long season, on growth of 3.5 m (11 ft). The unusual 'Handel' has large, fragrant, cream flowers flushed and edged pink, continuously borne, and glossy foliage. Its height is 4 m (13 ft).

Among coral pink roses you could choose, for a pillar, 'Dreamgirl,' with very fragrant, late-borne flowers of rosette shape; or the slightly taller 'Coral Dawn', its full blooms continuously borne. One of the most famous climbing pink roses, in its day, was 'Madame Edouard Herriot, Clg', also known as the Daily Mail rose. It is a fragrant, coral pink and apricot loose double rose of shortish growth and is still well worth a place if you appreciate the sunset colours.

Another old favourite of a pretty shade of pink is 'Shot Silk, Clg'. The bright salmon pink blooms with yellow base are fragrant and recurrent. It grows to about 3 m (10 ft). 'Compassion' is a much more modern rose of similar dimensions. Its high-centred, fragrant blooms are salmon flushed with apricot, set off by glossy foliage.

A rose with a difference in the large-flowered category is 'Meg'. A good pillar rose at 3 m (10 ft) or so, it has single apricot, fragrant blooms, and glossy foliage. 'Schoolgirl', with fully double coppery orange, fragrant blooms borne continuously, is brighter in colour.

The coming of the yellow roses

As we shall see later, the yellow climbing roses of the nineteenth century were generally shaded with peach or apricot. Pure lemon yellows arrived at the start of the twentieth century. The superb 'Paul's Lemon Pillar', dating from 1915, is very pale yellow, more like lemon sorbet than the fresh fruit. It has huge, fragrant HT blooms of lemon white, on stout growth up to 4.5 m (15 ft), in summer. Despite its name, 'Easlea's Golden Rambler' is a large-flowered climber, summer-flowering, with yellow, fragrant blooms, and very good foliage. It is tall, up to 6 m (20 ft), Another with great vigour is 'Lawrence Johnston', its large semi-double rich yellow, fragrant flowers borne in summer.

If you want a shorter-growing yellow rose, up to 2.5 m (8 ft), try 'Golden Showers', with double clear yellow, sweetly fragrant blooms continuously borne, and glossy foliage; or 'Leverkusen', with clear citron yellow double flowers in summer, fragrant of lemons, and pale foliage.

White climbing roses

Really good white climbing roses with large flowers are not many. An old one, yet with a modern look, is 'Madame Alfred Carrière'. A Noisette, it has white or palest blush, full, very fragrant flowers borne continuously. It does well on a shaded wall, growing to 4 m (13 ft).

The early hybrid tea 'Mrs Herbert Stevens, Clg' has elegant scrolled white blooms, with a tea fragrance, and a repeat season. It too grows to about 4 m (13 ft). For a shorter white climbing rose, there is a choice of two newer varieties: 'Swan Lake', with white HT blooms suffused blush pink, borne continuously, and with dark foliage. It is a good pillar rose. So too is 'White Cockade', with fully double pure white, fragrant blooms all season, and good foliage.

THE OLD AND THE NEW RAMBLERS

The very name 'rambler rose' is evocative, suggesting long stems weaving through a supporting tree or hedgerow, displaying clusters of many small flowers, quite different in character from the long, elegant blooms of the large-flowered roses. Except for a few vivid pink or crimson ramblers, the colours are soft: white, blush, buff yellow, mauve-pink with lavender shadings, tawny pink. Though the individual blooms cannot bear comparison, the ramblers' generosity of flower, coming from mid summer onwards when other favourites such as lilacs and rhododendrons are over, far surpasses that of the large-flowered climbers.

Many are deliciously fragrant also, thanks to their musk rose parentage. The wild musks will be described in the next section of this chapter; here I want to suggest some of the garden ramblers that have a place in our gardens and in our hearts. These, above all, are the roses to grow on pergolas, along fences and informal hedgerows, through the branches of trees. They can smother arbours and conceal sheds. They are least successful as wall plants, though even here their generosity accords well with cottage architecture.

Once-flowering ramblers are pruned after flowering, when the old flowered wood is cut out at the base. By this time there will usually be a mass of new shoots springing from the base, which are trained in as replacements. Those that give a repeat crop of flowers after mid summer generally produce fewer basal stems each year. These are pruned by cutting out some of the 2–3 year old wood each year.

Apple-scented flowers

Among the finest ramblers are those with fragrant, often apple-scented flowers and glossy foliage on branching growth, that need not be pruned each year. Typical of these is 'Albéric Barbier', which has pointed primrose yellow buds opening to quartered, ivory flowers with sweet apple scent. Scattered blooms appear after the main summer flush. It is vigorous in growth to 6 m (20 ft). Another is 'Albertine', a famous cottage favourite with tawny pink flowers, powerfully fragrant, in summer only, on strong thorny growths to 5.5 m (18 ft).

This coppery salmon colouring is found also in 'François Juranville', superior to 'Albertine', with apple-scented flowers in summer. It makes less shrubby, sometimes leggy growth to 6 m (20 ft). 'Paul Transon', which has flat double flowers of coral pink and salmon with a rich apple fragrance, is valued for being almost a recurrent bloomer. It reaches 4.5 m (15 ft). Also in this group is 'Emily Gray'. Warm yellow, nearly single, fragrant flowers are borne in summer. She is a vigorous rose reaching to 6 m (20 ft).

Clustered posies

For another rambling rose with yellow flowers, we can turn to a different kind of rambler, where the blood of *Rosa multiflora* brings a rich fruity fragrance and

Opposite: (*upper*): *Roses are grown above all for their flowers, but apple-scented 'Albéric Barbier' also has fine glossy foliage. The creamy flowers open over a long season from scrolled, yellow buds, a soft colour scheme that looks as well on grey stone as on warm red brick.*

Opposite (*lower*): Rosa banksiae *'Lutea' is the most popular of the Banksian roses, slightly tender climbers with almost thornless stems and abundant clusters of little posies. Where frosts are rare, the double yellow Banksian rose will fill a sizeable tree, to make a spectacular spring picture.*

clusters of many smallish flowers. 'Goldfinch' has yellow buds fading to primrose-ivory, very fragrant button flowers in clusters, in summer. The glossy light green foliage is borne on almost thornless stems of up to 2.5 m (8 ft).

Also of *R. multiflora* style is 'Blush Rambler', a very pretty old rambler bearing semi-double, pale pink, richly fragrant blooms in summer, amid pale foliage on almost thornless stems growing to 4.5 m (15 ft). 'Phyllis Bide' bears a long succession of double, salmon yellow, fragrant flowers in clusters, and reaches 4 m (13 ft). Very like a large-flowered *R. multiflora*, 'Seagull' has semi-double white flowers with yellow stamens and a terrific fragrance, borne in large clusters in summer. It is a good rambler for a tree, reaching 6 m (20 ft).

Different again is 'Adélaïde d'Orléans'. Its hanging clusters of double blush-pink flowers, opening from rosy buds, make it ideal for a pergola. Once-flowering, it makes growth up to 4.5 m (15 ft). It tends to be evergreen, as does 'Félicité et Perpétue', but this is a very bushy, late-flowering rambler, with abundant clusters of fragrant ivory rosettes. It is very hardy and tolerant of shade, and may reach 5.5 m. 'Francis E. Lester' is similar in growth, but very different in rich fruity-perfumed flower, wide clusters of pink buds opening to white with yellow stamens. It flowers only in summer but bears orange hips in autumn.

The blue ramblers

Although modern rose growers have been searching for a 'blue' rose, this colour — actually parma violet or purple — has been known in rambler roses for almost a century. By growing four different varieties you can keep this colour in the garden for weeks. First to open is 'Veilchenblau', the only fragrant 'blue' rambler, with clusters of magenta purple blooms fading to violet and lilac, often white-streaked, amid fresh green foliage. Its height is around 4 m (13 ft). It is closely followed by 'Violette', which is actually crimson purple fading to maroon and lilac. It is a little taller at 4.5 m (15 ft).

Next it is the turn of 'Rose-Marie Viaud', with rosettes of cerise and purple fading to parma violet, no scent and few thorns. This too reaches 4.5 m (15 ft). Lastly, 'Bleu Magenta', with purple flowers fading to violet and grey. It lacks fragrance, but has the largest and deepest violet-purple flowers. It grows to 4 m.

Either of these is delightful with 'Kew Rambler', which bears bright pink, richly fragrant single flowers with a white eye. They are set off by greyish foliage. A tall grower to 5.5 m (18 ft), it looks well in a tree.

Edwardian ramblers

For arches and trellis, to create a period effect, you could choose 'Dorothy Perkins', still very popular for its clusters of small pink, scarcely scented flowers. It grows to 5.5 m (18 ft), as does its crimson counterpart 'Excelsa'. 'Crimson Shower' is of richer crimson colouring, a late-starting, long-flowering rose with little scent. It is a little less tall, at 4.5 m (15 ft).

'Débutante' can be used in the same way. It is a very pretty pink fading to blush, fragrant, once-flowering rambler, with glossy foliage on stems up to 4.5 m (15 ft). 'Sanders' White Rambler' is excellent also on a pergola; it resembles

'Dorothy Perkins' in habit, but has pure white flowers with a fruity fragrance.

'Weetwood' is a promising new rambler, with pale pink rosette flowers in large hanging clusters. It may perhaps reach 6 m (20 ft). With roses like these available, surely we could discard 'American Pillar', unless you like its triumphantly vulgar single vivid pink flowers with white eye, borne in summer only. It is all too vigorous at 4.5 m (15 ft).

Much more appealing than this is 'Spectabilis', an old rose dating from before 1848, with hanging clusters of creamy lilac rosettes, sweetly fragrant, late in the season. It is a modest little rose growing to 2 m (6 ft).

MUSK ROSES — THE FRAGRANT GIANTS

These are the original species, and some garden varieties very near to them in character, from which the old and new garden ramblers derive, and indeed ultimately many of our garden roses whether climbing or shrubby. They are also known as the Synstylae roses; for the botanically minded, this is because the bunch of styles in the centre of each flower is packed into a column, not spread out as in other roses. From the gardener's point of view, they are mostly vigorous, some even rampant growers, almost all with white or cream flowers in large clusters, and delectably fragrant with a far-carrying perfume. Reginald Farrer describes how their fragrance in the wild carried 'for half a mile... in every direction'. So you will see that they have no difficulty filling the average garden with scent.

Their vigour makes them ideal for growing into trees. Some will need large trees; others will fit an old apple or pear tree or a cherry. They flower once, usually at mid summer. Some have bunches of little bright orange or red hips to follow their flowers in an autumn display. On the whole these musk roses need little pruning unless you are growing them on a wall, when you may need to thin and tidy them by removing old and twiggy stems, and any that are diseased or not flowering with the usual musk rose generosity.

The musk rose of Shakespeare

Rosa arvensis may be the rose Shakespeare wrote about as 'sweet musk roses', but it is only for the wild garden for it is almost uncontrollable. Dark leaves set off creamy, fragrant flowers in high summer. Much more garden-worthy is *Rosa brunonii*, the Himalayan musk rose. It has elegant greyish foliage, but the flower clusters are rather tight. The form 'La Mortola' has finer blooms and is equally fragrant, but a little tender in cold climates. At 9–12 m it needs plenty of room.

'Rambling Rector' is also called 'Shakespeare's Musk', though it may not be the real thing. However, it is a wonderful rose, with cream flowers fading to white, in huge quantities, with a terrific perfume and vigour, at 7.5 m (25 ft).

These need ample space

The word vigour will often occur when these musk roses are described, but never more than with *Rosa filipes*. A huge rose, it has tinted young foliage and clusters of

100 or more white flowers on thread-like stalks, very fragrant and borne rather late in the season. This is the form known as 'Kiftsgate'. Another is 'Brenda Colvin', similar except the flowers are blush pink fading to white. 'Treasure Trove' also has growth similar to 'Kiftsgate', but the flowers are rosettes of creamy apricot, in clusters.

Another very vigorous grower — 9 m (30 ft) — is 'Paul's Himalayan Musk'. Double rosettes of blush lilac flowers in hanging clusters are borne at mid summer on slender stems. Although a very generous rose, 'Bobbie James' is slightly more restrained at about 6 m. It has glossy foliage and wide heads of creamy flowers.

You need plenty of space, again, for 'Wedding Day'. A 10.5 m (35 ft) hybrid of *R. sinowilsonii*, it has glossy foliage and large clusters of starry ivory flowers, richly scented of oranges. Rain brings the petals out in pink blotches. *Rosa sinowilsonii* itself is rather tender, and has not the best flowers in the group, but beautiful foliage, dark green above and shining maroon-red beneath. Allow 9 m at least.

Also from China, *Rosa helenae* is distinguished by fierce hooked prickles. The rounded clusters of creamy flowers, against dark green foliage, are followed by very showy hips. It grows to 6 m (20 ft), and I have seen it as a huge lax shrub much wider than high. You could try the same treatment for *Rosa longicuspis*. Late flowering, this has glossy foliage tinted when young, and cream buds opening to ivory flowers in clusters of 150 or more, with a rich fruity fragrance. Tiny hips follow.

Fruity fragrance

Rosa multiflora, ancestor of many ramblers, has already been mentioned. Much used as a stock for budding, it is beautiful in its own right with single milk-white flowers, and a tremendous fruity fragrance. In autumn it bears bright red pea-sized hips. Its very dense growth up to 6 m (20 ft) as a rambler makes it suitable as a loose shrub in a hedgerow. *Rosa multiflora* 'Platyphylla' (correctly called 'Grevillei') is the seven sisters rose, so called because each cluster of flower shows many different colours from cerise and purple to mauve and cream. It has a fresh fragrance and grows to 5.5 m (18 ft).

'Polyantha Grandiflora' is the familiar name for *Rosa gentiliana*. Its creamy flowers and showy yolk yellow stamens at mid summer mature into long-lasting orange-red hips, on stems up to 6 m (20 ft). An unusual, and rather more re-strained, rose in this group is 'The Garland'. Its very fragrant flowers, with quilled daisy-like petals, cream opening from salmon buds, are always held erect.

The name *Rosa wichuriana* used to be much used to describe a certain style of rambler. A trailing evergreen rose, it is indeed the parent of many ramblers. The domed clusters of white flowers are borne in late summer. If trained upwards into a tree it will cascade down most gracefully. It can reach 4.5 m (15 ft).

ROSES FOR SHELTERED WALLS

The roses I shall describe next have in common that in a cold climate they need a sheltered wall to give of their best. Some of them are more tender than others. 'Gloire de Dijon', for example, is not really a tender rose at all, but it belongs in

'Zéphyrine Drouhin' is one of the best pillar or pole roses, perpetual-flowering, thornless and richly fragrant. The bright, cake-icing pink flowers glow with an unexpected fiery warmth in the fading light of evening.

the same group as several other climbing roses that do need shelter. Then there is the Banksian rose, distinctly less hardy, but in Mediterranean-style climates it can be grown in tall trees or as a great flopping bush, as well as on a wall.

The Noisette roses

Several of these roses belong to a group known as the Noisettes (from the name of the nurseryman who raised the first). They have blood of the original old tea roses in them, as well as the China roses. Some of the climbing teas themselves also belong here, and an exquisite race known as the tea Noisettes, with flowers of tender shades of yellow. There would be few climbers more lovely to collect, if one had plenty of wall space, than these old yellow roses.

The most famous of them all is 'Gloire de Dijon'. The old glory rose, long-flowering and opulent in buff yellow flushed with peach, and richly scented, will reach 5.5 m (18 ft). It does very well on a part-shaded wall. One of its offspring is 'Bouquet d'Or', which bears large full flowers of warm salmon with a yellow centre. It has less fragrance, and is of shorter growth to 3 m (10 ft). 'Paul Lédé, Clg' is like a richer coloured, even more sweetly scented 'Gloire de Dijon', growing to 4.5 m (15 ft).

One of the earliest Noisettes to be raised was 'Desprez à Fleur Jaune'. It is still treasured for its beautiful double flowers of creamy peach flushed yellow, power-fully fragrant and very perpetual, on growth up to 4.5 m (15 ft). It was not, however, the very first; that honour goes to 'Blush Noisette', introduced before 1817. It bears a continuous succession of clusters of cupped old-rose flowers fading to blush-lilac, with rich clove fragrance, on almost thornless growth to 4.5 m (15 ft). A few years later came 'Aimée Vibert' which bears clusters of full white flowers from pink tipped buds, from high summer until autumn; well sheltered it starts flowering in early summer. It has glossy foliage and reaches 4.5 m.

One of the most perpetual of Noisettes is 'Alister Stella Gray'. Its scrolled yellow buds open to flat, quartered flowers held in small sprays in summer and great branching heads in autumn. They are very fragrant and make enchanting buttonholes. Despite the petite appearance of the flowers, this rose grows to 4.5 m (15 ft). 'Claire Jacquier' is similar to 'Alister Stella Gray', but a good bit taller, hardier and not so perpetual. In cool climates at least, 'Céline Forestier' is of most modest growth at 2.5 m (8 ft). The flat, quartered flowers of primrose yellow, with peach tints at first, have a delicious tea scent and are borne in long succession.

'William Allen Richardson' is a strange Noisette with unique apricot-orange flowers, fading to near-white in hot sun. It has maroon young foliage on angular growth to 4 m (13 ft).

Others among the yellow Noisettes really do need warmth and shelter. 'Rêve d'Or' has loosely double, buff yellow and apricot flowers continuously borne, and endowed with a slight fragrance. It will reach 3 m (10 ft). The exquisite 'Lamarque' has very double flat nodding flowers, lemon white to ivory, with a sweet tea scent. It is recurrent and grows to 3 m (10 ft). The most tender of all is 'Maréchal Niel', a sumptuous rose with shapely, nodding flowers of soft yellow and a delicious tea scent. In cold climates it needs conservatory protection and is unlikely to exceed 3 m (10 ft).

The climbing teas

These deserve cossetting with warmth and shelter. 'Devoniensis, Clg' is known as the 'magnolia rose' for its very large creamy flowers at first flushed apricot, fragrant and recurrent. It will grow to 3 m (10 ft) or more. When fully open, 'Sombreuil, Clg' has even flatter, quartered, creamy flowers tinted with peach at the heart, and a sweet tea scent; it is recurrent, and reaches 4 m (13 ft). 'Lady Hillingdon, Clg' displays the high-centred, scrolled flower shape first encountered in the teas and transmitted to the hybrid teas. The apricot yellow, fragrant, recurrent flowers are set off by plum purple young foliage. This too grows to 4 m.

The Banksian roses

The Banksian roses are vigorous but rather tender climbers growing to 6 m (20 ft) or more, almost thornless, with green stems and light green foliage. The clusters of little flowers of *Rosa banksiae* are borne in late spring. Single and double forms in both white and yellow are known. The most familiar is 'Lutea', the double yellow; it is less fragrant than the others. Little or no pruning is needed unless to keep them in bounds when old stems, five years old or more, should be cut right out.

Similar but larger flowers are borne by *Rosa × fortuneana*, a cross between the Banksian rose and *R. laevigata*. The fully double, creamy white blooms open early in the season. This too is for warm gardens only.

Wild roses from China

Rosa laevigata itself is known as the Cherokee rose, for it is naturalized in the United States and adopted as the state flower of Georgia, but it is a native of China. Nearly evergreen, with dark polished leaves, it needs a sheltered wall or a warm climate. The large single flowers, creamy white and very fragrant, open in late spring, on vigorous growths to 7.5 m (25 ft). *Rosa laevigata* 'Cooperi' or Cooper's Burmese rose is a very fine form, even taller at 10.5 m (35 ft).

The Cherokee rose has two beautiful descendants in 'Anemone', with large single flowers of soft clear pink, silvery reverse, over a long season, and its deeper sport 'Ramona', its cerise, single flowers backed with fawn to grey. Both flower early and long, and grow to 2.5 m (8 ft).

Rosa bracteata, the Macartney rose from China, is rather more tender. Its silky white single flowers with bright orange stamens, lemon-scented, appear from summer to autumn amid very dark green glossy foliage. Allow 4.5 m (15 ft) for this, but almost twice as much for its offspring 'Mermaid'. Though slightly tender, this flowers well even on sunless walls. The large, single, clear yellow flowers, with showy amber stamens, are continuously borne.

THE REST OF THE CLIMBING ROSES

Inevitably, not every rose will fit into a convenient pigeonhole. There are several climbers too good to omit that I group here, though they are of different kinds.

Some of the Bourbon roses, usually shrubby, can be trained as climbers. One of the most famous is 'Zéphyrine Drouhin'. Half a climber, half a shrub, growing to 3 m (10 ft), it is very perpetual, with loosely double, cake-icing pink flowers, incandescent at dusk, and richly fragrant. It has a shorter-growing sport in 'Kathleen Harrop', with charming shell pink flowers. Both are ideal pole roses. 'Souvenir de la Malmaison, Clg' has flat, quartered blooms, blush white shaded with powder pink, fragrant and recurrent. It is taller, at 4 m (13 ft). 'Blairii No. 2' has large flat, full-petalled, fragrant blooms of pale pink with deeper centre, in summer. At 4.5 m it is the tallest of the group.

Some people call 'Zéphyrine Drouhin' the thornless rose, as though all others had prickles. However, another that has stems without prickles is 'Madame Sancy de Parabère'. A Boursault rose, it has large, clear pink flowers, the central petals forming a rosette surrounded by larger outer petals, borne very early in the season on growth up to 4.5 m (15 ft).

Two very different climbers are sometimes described as miniature. In the case of 'Cécile Brunner, Clg', it is the perfect HT blooms that are miniature, small enough to fit in a thimble, the scrolled buds opening to clear pink, chiefly at mid summer. It has a sweet fragrance and makes vigorous growth to 6 m (20 ft). 'Pompon de Paris' is miniature in growth, a China rose with twiggy stems to 2.5 m (8 ft), tiny leaves and little button rosettes of bright pink, in summer.

6
CLEMATIS

CLEMATIS, AS WE HAVE SEEN, complement climbing roses. Like climbing roses, they come in a wide range of styles from the large-flowered hybrids, triumphs of the breeders' art, to untamed wildlings. As with roses, by choosing your varieties carefully you can have a long season of clematis blooms. Clematis are weak on fragrance, it is true, although there are some scented kinds, but they bring a range of colours lacking in the roses. The near-blues, the rich purples and violets, the gentle lavender and lilac tones of clematis are unmatched among roses. The pinker tones of mauve clematis — there is no true, pure pink among the large-flowered hybrids — have a soft, old-fashioned charm that is very much in harmony with the older roses.

Many clematis, like some climbing roses, have a tendency to legginess. On walls, their bare legs can be hidden by growing them among shrubs: evergreen wall shrubs will give a solidity lacking in the clematis.

Like roses, clematis can also be grown in more natural ways, among shrubs and into trees, as well as on garden structures: pergolas, arches, trellis. Their flexible stems, with twining leafstalks, give them an easy purchase on twiggy supports, but they will need tying in to frameworks of stouter construction. Some people fix clematis netting around the uprights of pergolas or on poles, but this is not very aesthetic, as clematis, the large-flowered kinds, at least, are seldom sufficiently leafy in summer to hide the netting, and in winter the bare stems reveal all.

Pruning clematis is far less complicated than beginners fear. It all comes down, with clematis as with other plants, to one question: does the clematis flower on last year's growths, or on the new ones of this season? Those that bear their flowers early in the season on last year's stems, classified below as Group 1, need pruning only if they outgrow their space, when you cut back flowered shoots immediately after flowering. This applies to the early spring-flowered species.

Among large-flowered clematis, and the small-flowered kinds that bloom in summer, there are two possibilities. Either they flower on last year's growths, starting in late spring (these are classed as Group 2), or they flower on new growths made this year (Group 3). Group 2 are lightly pruned: dead stems are cut right out, and healthy ones trimmed back just to the topmost plump bud, in late winter. Group 3 are cut hard back, also in late winter, to 1 m (3 ft) or less from

Opposite: *The grey, rugged bark of a tree shows off the pink blooms of* Clematis *'Comtesse de Bouchaud'. Many clematis, both large-flowered and small, can be grown in this informal way, as well as on walls or trellis. A cane leads the clematis stems to the fork in the trunk, and thereafter just a little discreet guidance should suffice.*

ground level; new shoots will quickly grow, to flower after mid summer. Some are obliging enough to fit into either Group 2 or Group 3, so if you make a mistake you need not panic.

Propagating clematis is not, on the whole, the baffling mystery sometimes imagined, either. Gone are the days when almost all clematis grown commercially were grafted; most are raised from cuttings, some from seed. On a small scale clematis can be increased by layering. However, even the amateur can be successful with clematis cuttings of almost all kinds except *C. armandii*, which is rather difficult to grow on successfully after it has made roots. The method is described in Chapter 4.

LARGE-FLOWERED CLEMATIS HYBRIDS

Just as I began with the familar roses with HT-style blooms, so I start with their counterparts, the large-flowered clematis hybrids. Though they match, even out-class, the large-flowered roses in floral display, these clematis are perhaps more adaptable, for they are as happy growing through and over host plants as they are on more formal supports — walls, trellis, pergolas. Like the roses, they are greedy feeders, preferring to have their roots shaded but generally happier with their heads in the sun. Unless your soil is excessively acid, they do not need added lime.

Between them, the large-flowered clematis span half the year, their earliest blooms opening before the first of the roses. Yet they derive originally from only four wild species, two of which were crossed to produce the famous *C. × jackmanii* in 1860. Clematis are long-lasting, so now there are both old and new varieties to choose from.

The Jackmanii clematis

Probably everyone who has the slightest interest in plants and in gardens knows 'Jackmanii Superba', that enduringly popular, tough and showy, velvety-purple clematis. Prune it as a Group 3 clematis, and expect it to grow to 4.5 m (15 ft). It has broad overlapping sepals of deep violet, with a reddish tinge at first, in summer. 'Jackmanii Alba' is not really, as its name seems to suggest, a white version, for it has double, skimmed-milk white flowers in late spring, rather ragged; the late summer flowers are single. For pruning purposes it falls into Group 2 or 3. The same is true of 'Jackmanii Rubra', which has double early flowers and single later in the season, of petunia red. The much newer 'John Huxtable' is in effect a white Jackmanii with cream anthers, flowering from summer to autumn. Prune it as Group 3, and expect it to reach 3 m (10 ft).

Striped clematis of 'Nelly Moser' style

Running the Jackmanii clematis close in familiarity is 'Nelly Moser', with mauve-pink flowers, each sepal marked with a bold carmine bar, like a 'stripey cartwheel', in the words of Christopher Lloyd, the clematis expert. Sepal? Well, clematis belong to the buttercup family and like others in the family — delphiniums and anemones, for example — the showy part of the flower is the calyx, formed of sepals. The petals, in such flowers, are inconspicuous or, as in *Clematis*, altogether missing. Virtually all the 'Nelly Moser' type clematis grow to around 3 m (10 ft) and are pruned as for Group 2. They all tend to fade in bright sun, and are therefore often recommended for lightly shaded positions or even sunless walls.

There are several other striped clematis of 'Nelly Moser' type. The two Barbaras are both fine clematis: 'Barbara Dibley' has big flowers of rich petunia red in late spring with late summer repeat but the flowers fade badly in sun; 'Barbara Jackman' is a better plant, its bright blue-purple sepals with carmine bar fading pleasantly. It flowers first in late spring, and has a late summer repeat, as is typical of Group 2 clematis.

Although broad, overlapping sepals are usually considered the ideal in large-flowered clematis, a starry flower has its charms too. 'Lincoln Star' comes bright raspberry pink in early summer; the later flowers are paler with carmine bar, showing off crimson anthers. Of slightly shorter growth is 'Bracebridge Star', in starry lavender with a carmine bar and red anthers, in early summer.

'Marcel Moser', in mauve-pink with carmine bar, has larger blooms than 'Nelly Moser', in early and late summer, and is perhaps less vigorous, needing good soil to do well. 'Bees Jubilee', mauve-pink with carmine bar, flowering in late spring and late summer, is reasonably vigorous but rather apt to suffer from wilt.

The most common colouring in the striped clematis is a ground tone of lavender pink or rosy mauve with brighter carmine bar. Both 'Sealand Gem', in pale rosy lavender with carmine bar soon fading, and 'Souvenir du Capitaine Thuilleaux', with a very broad carmine bar on pale lilac-pink sepals, are of this colouring. The first has very freely borne, medium-sized blooms, from summer to autumn; the second flowers chiefly in summer and can be pruned as for Group 2 or 3. 'Dr Ruppel' is another of basically rosy mauve tones, the large flowers with deep carmine bar and chocolate anthers, opening in late spring and autumn.

'Scartho Gem' is very free-flowering in bright pink with deeper carmine bar, over a long season from summer to autumn, so that it can be classed as Group 2 or 3. A newer variety is 'Carnaby', in raspberry pink with deeper carmine bar, starting into flower in early summer. It grows to only 2 m (6 ft) or so.

Then there is 'Mrs N. Thompson'. She has showy deep violet blooms with bright carmine bar and purple stamens, in early summer and autumn.

Red clematis

The 'red' clematis, which are actually rich magenta, wine or velvety crimson-purple in colour, look well with fuchsias, and the later flowers in this range make a startling blend with the bright mauve fruits of *Callicarpa* and the petunia-purple plumes of *Lespedeza thunbergii*, with nerines or pink colchicums at their feet. Buddleias, purple gladioli and the deeper-toned Michaelmas daisies also fit well in such schemes, with silvery or grey foliage.

In this colour range, 'Ville de Lyon' is a famous old vivid carmine-red clematis with cream stamens. It needs generous treatment and light pruning to flower from late spring to autumn. It can be treated as Group 2 or 3, and should reach 3 m

(10 ft). Hardly less renowned is 'Ernest Markham', which bears vivid magenta blooms from mid summer to autumn. Another of the obliging Group 2 or 3 clematis, it grows to 4 m (13 ft).

Neither 'Duchess of Sutherland' nor 'Crimson King' is as easy-going as this, needing good cultivation to thrive. The first is one of the finest reds when doing well, with large, well-shaped blooms of crimson-carmine, from mid to late summer. Treat it as Group 2 or 3, when it should grow to 3 m (10 ft). 'Crimson King' is a bright crimson-red with brown stamens, flowering all summer, and definitely in Group 2.

Flower texture may be as important as colour. Among the reds, 'Madame Edouard André' is matt textured, of dusky wine-red with cream stamens. It has one abundant, two-month summer season and should be pruned as for Group 3. So much flower means it is not very vigorous, reaching 2 m (6 ft). By contrast, 'Rouge Cardinal' has velvety deep crimson blooms with pale stamens, in summer. It is best in sun, and grows much like 'Madame Ed. André', as she is known in the trade. The brighter, wine-red 'Allanah', flowering from mid to late summer, is another of these dimensions and style.

The last three reds I want to mention all grow to around 3 m (10 ft) and are pruned as for Group 3. 'Voluceau' has petunia-red flowers with yellow stamens, very freely borne from summer to autumn. 'Cardinal Wyszynski', crimson with yellow stamens, has fairly large flowers over a long summer season. Perhaps the most appealing, though far from the brightest, is 'Niobe'. The deep velvety maroon-red, sun-proof blooms need a light background for best effect.

Pink and mauve clematis

Mauve-pink clematis make softer harmonies, with pink or mauve-toned old roses, the glaucous and plum leaves of *Rosa glauca* (*R. rubrifolia*), purple sage and pink Japanese anemones, nepeta, pink phloxes and pink *Lavatera olbia* (tree mallow).

Probably the best mauve-pink variety is 'Comtesse de Bouchaud'. She is of *jackmanii* style, very free-flowering at mid summer, falling into Group 3, and growing to 3 m (10 ft). 'Hagley Hybrid' is another good clematis, compact at 2.5 m (8 ft) and free-flowering from mid summer to autumn. The blooms are dusky mauve-pink with dark stamens. Prune as for Group 3.

The two Kathleens are both of this colouring, though 'Kathleen Dunford', which has semi-double flowers in late spring and single in autumn, is a rather dim shade of rosy purple to magenta. A Group 2 clematis, she grows to 3m (10 ft). 'Kathleen Wheeler' is a better plant, with abundant large flowers of rosy mauve with showy yellow stamens, in summer. Also in Group 2, she is more compact at 2.5 m (8 ft).

A newer Group 2 clematis in this colouring is 'Pink Champagne' ('Kakio'), which has large blooms of lavender-pink with pale central bar and creamy stamens, borne in early and late summer. Its height is 3 m (10 ft) or so. 'John Warren' is one of those obliging Group 2 or 3 varieties, good for small spaces as it reaches only 2 m (6 ft). The lilac-pink blooms, fading to French grey, have carmine margins and midribs, and open from summer to autumn.

Some later clematis, falling into Group 3, need sun and warmth if they are to flower. Such is 'Madame Baron Veillard', which bears warm lilac-rose, smallish flowers in autumn. She is vigorous in growth to 4 m (13 ft). So too is 'Margaret Hunt'. This dusky mauve-pink clematis, with neatly symmetrical flowers, blooms in high summer and does not depend on a sunny autumn to perform well. 'Twilight', which bears carmine-rose blooms fading to soft mauve-pink from summer to autumn, grows to 3 m (10 ft).

Some pink clematis are so pale as to be almost white. 'Dawn', as befits its name, flowers earlier than 'Twilight', in late spring and late summer, putting it in Group 2. The pearly blush, wide blooms with carmine anthers, are borne on growth to 3 m (10 ft). 'Fair Rosamond' (Group 2, again, and much the same height as 'Dawn') has scented blush white flowers with pink bar and purple stamens, in summer. You will need more space for 'John Paul II', which grows to 4.5 m (15 ft). From summer to autumn appear its white flowers tinged with pink, sometimes forming a distinct bar on later blooms.

The refinement of white

Among true whites, there is one name that stands out: 'Marie Boisselot' ('Madame le Coultre'). This famous white clematis bears large, full and well-presented blooms with ivory stamens, all summer, on stems up to 4 m (13 ft). You can treat her as Group 2 or 3. 'Henryi', by contrast, has dark stamens to its large starry white flowers, opening from summer to autumn amid bronzed foliage. Group 2 pruning suits it best, and it grows to 4 m (13 ft).

'Edith' needs similar treatment, but reaches only 3 m (10 ft), The large ice-white flowers with dark anthers are borne from early to late summer. Another quite new clematis of this type, which grows to only 2 m (6 ft), is 'Gillian Blades'. It bears fairly large white flowers faintly edged in mauve, with yellow stamens, in early summer and autumn. 'Miss Bateman' is an older clematis of similar size and style, with creamy-white, well-formed flowers with hints of green, and red anthers, in early summer. 'Snow Queen', similar again in requirements, is not as white as the name suggests, for the flowers are tinged with blue in early summer, and the autumn blooms sometimes have a pink bar.

If you want a white clematis as adaptable to Group 2 or 3 pruning as 'Marie Boisselot', but only half as tall, choose 'Mrs George Jackman'. Her creamy white blooms, with broad overlapping sepals and buff stamens, sometimes come semi-double. Her season is early to late summer.

I really have to include the large-flowered yellow clematis here, for they are as pale as primroses or clotted cream, scarcely yellow at all. 'Yellow Queen' ('Moonlight'), in pale primrose with creamy anthers, needs light shade. It flowers in summer, putting it in Group 2, and grows to 2 m (6 ft), 'Wada's Primrose', in palest primrose to cream, differs in growing twice as tall.

Nearest to blue

'Blue' clematis, as we have seen, contrast tenderly with yellow or with pink roses, or mingle with shrubs of off-blue such as *Caryopteris*, and with silvery foliage.

There is no pure blue clematis, of course; but I use the word to distinguish those nearest to blue from lavender or violet clematis. One of the most striking is 'Lasurstern'. Its rich blue, wide flowers with prominent ivory stamens are borne in early and late summer. It can therefore be treated as Group 2 or 3, and grows to 3 m (10 ft). 'Lady Northcliffe' behaves similarly, bearing near-blue flowers composed of broad wavy sepals with whitish anthers all summer. She is good for small spaces, reaching only 2 m (6 ft).

Another richly coloured blue clematis of similar size and flowering habits is 'Elsa Späth'. The purple-blue, large flowers have purple anthers. The blooms of 'Lord Nevill' have deep purple sepals with wavy margins, and appear over a long summer season. This is a little taller, at 3m (10 ft).

'Richard Pennell,' of similar rich purple-blue colouring with yellow and red stamens, flowers in summer, and should be treated as Group 2. It reaches 3 m (10 ft). Earlier in the season you can have much the same colouring from 'Etoile de Paris'. The deep purple-blue, starry flowers, fading fast, are borne on growth of 2 m (6 ft).

Other Group 2 clematis — flowering, that is, from early summer or even late spring — are mainly mid-blue in colour. 'H. F. Young' has refined blooms with cream stamens, with a second crop in autumn, and grows to 2.5 m (8 ft). The flowers of 'General Sikorski', in mid-blue tinged with red, have crimpled edges and yellow stamens. It reaches 3 m (10 ft). 'Mrs P. B. Truax' is always described as periwinkle blue with creamy anthers, a fine clematis growing to 3 m (10 ft).

Those that will flower on both young and old wood, making them adaptable to either Group 2 or Group 3 pruning, include 'Mrs Hope', whose large, full porcelain blue flowers with maroon stamens are borne from summer to autumn on stems up to 4 m (13 ft), and the tall (4.5 m [15 ft]) 'William Kennett', in deep lavender-blue with red-purple bar and maroon stamens. Then there is the admirable 'Mrs Cholmondeley', very free-flowering, with large rather starry Wedgwood blue blooms from late spring to autumn, growing to 4 m (13 ft) tall.

Among the true summer-flowering clematis of Group 3, there are two blues to choose from. 'Ascotiensis' is the earlier, a good mid-blue variety flowering from mid summer, but it has not a well-shaped flower. It grows to only 2.5 m (8 ft) or so. The outstanding blue clematis, however, is 'Perle d'Azur'. A superb porcelain blue clematis of *C. × jackmanii* style, it bears abundant mid-sized blooms all summer on 4 m (13 ft) growth. If you can have only one clematis in your garden, it must be this.

Violet and purple clematis

Any pale foliage, whether grey or white-variegated, makes a stunning backdrop for violet-purple clematis. Another way with them is to make rich Byzantine mixtures of reds and purples and violets with coppery foliage and daring touches of scarlet.

I will begin with the Group 2 clematis in this colour, those that flower from late spring or early summer. One of the finest is 'The President', which bears three crops, from late spring on, of cupped blue-purple flowers with silvery reverse. The young leaves are bronzed. It is of medium height at 3 m (10 ft). 'Haku Ookan', a Japanese variety with violet, white-centred blooms in late spring and autumn, is shorter at 2.5 m (8 ft). The bushy, 2 m (6 ft) growth of 'Maureen' needs little pruning. Violet-purple, full flowers are borne in summer. Of similar height but more conventional growth, 'Percy Picton' commemorates a great plantsman; it has large purple blooms fading to intense mauve, in summer.

'Corona', in purple suffused pink, with dark red anthers, is free-flowering in early and late summer, and compact in growth to 2 m (6 ft). You can prune this as Group 2 or 3. So too with the 3 m (10 ft) 'Serenata', which bears dusky purple blooms with a deeper bar and primrose stamens, from summer to autumn.

The remainder I shall describe among the purples are all Group 3, flowering no earlier than high summer and some well into autumn. Among the summer starters is the oddly named 'Lilacina Floribunda' ('Guiding Star'). Rich purple, to me, does not equate with the word 'Lilacina'. Its season is summer to early autumn, its height 4 m (13 ft). 'Victoria' is of similar dimensions, its light purple flowers with deeper bar fading to mauve and opening all summer. Then there is the fine 'Star of India', a clematis of *C. × jackmanii* type, the purple blooms with a deep carmine-plum bar, during a summer to autumn season.

'Gipsy Queen' bears well-formed velvety purple blooms with dark stamens from late summer to autumn, and grows strongly to 4.5 m (15 ft). The purple-maroon 'Madame Grangé' has incurved sepals showing a pewter reverse. It too flowers from late summer to autumn, and reaches 3 m (10 ft). Latest of them all, needing sun and warmth in cold gardens and high latitudes to flower at all, is 'Lady Betty Balfour'. She bears strong purple blooms with cream stamens in autumn. She does not lack vigour, growing to 4.5 m (15 ft).

Lavender and blue-mauve clematis

These are the clematis that fall between the 'blues' and the pinky mauves. They go well with the softer yellows, say with a rose such as 'Golden Showers' rather than the buff to apricot tones of the Noisettes. Lavender clematis also look well with most shades of pink and will make a blue-pink rose seem clearer in colour. They make for gentle, rather than startling, colour harmonies.

'Lawsoniana', an old variety, has still the largest flowers of all, of rosy lavender fading towards blue, in summer. Prune as for Group 2, and expect it to grow to 3 m (10 ft). Another with very large flowers is 'Empress of India'. It has light violet blooms with deeper bar, in summer, falling also into Group 2, but more compact at 2.5 m (8 ft). The flowers of 'Horn of Plenty', large and cupped, are at first rosy mauve fading towards blue, opening during late spring and autumn. It should reach 3 m (10 ft). So too will 'Hybrida Sieboldiana' ('Ramona'), another Group 2 clematis with large lavender-blue flowers in summer.

'Lady Londesborough' is one of the first in this group to open, its palest lavender-mauve flowers fading to silvery-grey, with red anthers. It too is of medium height at 3 m (10 ft). 'Mrs Bush' follows at mid summer, displaying deep lavender-blue, large flowers, with chocolate anthers, on growth to 3 m (10 ft). Unlike these, 'Prins Hendrick' is a show variety rather than a garden clematis. It bears very large lavender-blue blooms, the sepals with crimped margins, in summer. For the garden, 'Will Goodwin' is a better choice, like a smaller-flowered 'Prins Hendrick' in pale lavender-blue with crinkled edges. It should reach 3 m (10 ft).

'Sir Garnet Wolseley' is a fine old clematis flowering from early summer, with deep lavender blooms and maroon stamens. He gives a good late summer crop, is pruned as Group 2, and grows to 3 m (10 ft). Although it has the same two-season blooming, 'Beauty of Richmond' can be treated as Group 2 or 3, but of course if the latter, will bear its large, pale lavender blooms only in late summer. It grows to some 3 m (10 ft). 'Silver Moon' is another of this kind, with pale lavender blooms fading to mauve, best out of the sun, from summer to autumn.

If you prune 'W. E. Gladstone' very lightly, you will get a long season of very large, silky lavender blooms with dark anthers, on 3 m (10 ft) growth. With 'Lady Caroline Nevill', you will get some semi-double blooms in late spring if you prune her lightly. Otherwise, she produces her lavender-blue flowers in summer, on vigorous growth to 4.5 m (15 ft).

'Belle Nantaise' is definitely a Group 3 clematis, with long, pointed lavender sepals and ivory anthers over a long summer season, on stems up to 2.5 m (8 ft).

Double-flowered clematis

Several varieties that tend to produce double flowers at their first, early-summer flowering, have been mentioned. But those that make a speciality of being double deserve to be described separately. Always, though, the later blooms on the young growths can be expected to be single. Pruning for double flowers should be as Group 2. They come in all the clematis colours, from white and mauve to the intense blue of 'Beauty of Worcester', which is very free-flowering. The autumn blooms, being single, display a white centre. The growth is moderate to 2.5 m (8 ft). Another of near-blue colouring is 'Countess of Lovelace', a clear lavender blue which needs generous feeding. Single flowers with cream anthers are borne in autumn, on 2.5 m (8 ft) growth.

Moving further from blue, there are the Pennells. 'Vyvyan Pennell' is very double, with a full centre and outer guard of broad sepals, in lilac and lavender-blue. The season is early summer, with single flowers in early autumn. 'Walter Pennell' is similar, the outer guard sepals with deep carmine bar. Both grow to 3 m (10 ft), as does 'Royalty', a double mauve-purple with yellow anthers in summer, single in autumn.

'Daniel Deronda' is a fine clematis with very large semi-double and single flowers of deep violet with paler bar down each sepal, borne over a long season on growth to 3 m (10 ft). 'Belle of Woking' is palest silvery-mauve, of double rosette form, blooming at mid summer and growing to 2.5 m (8 ft).

Opposite
'Frances Rivis' has the largest flowers of the Clematis alpina *group. In the European Alps, this dainty clematis scrambles through shrubs and among rocks, but you would need a very large rock garden to emulate this at home. Many garden shrubs, however, would host a* Clematis alpina.

The finest of the 'pink' double clematis is 'Proteus'. An old and unbeaten variety, this has double, mauve-pink blooms, as full as a peony, in early summer (autumn blooms single), on strong growth to 4 m (13 ft). 'Miss Crawshay' is less ample, a semi-double lilac-pink with fawn stamens, flowering in early summer on stems to 3 m (10 ft). The taller 'Mrs Spencer Castle', in pale lilac-pink, should perhaps have been mentioned earlier, for she sometimes fails to produce her double, early summer blooms altogether.

The old 'Duchess of Edinburgh' is a full double white with a tendency, admired by some and abhorred by others, to greenish tints around creamy anthers. She flowers in summer and grows to 3 m (10 ft). The newer 'Sylvia Denny' is a semi-double white with primrose anthers, blooming in early and late summer on growth to 3 m (10 ft).

SPRING-FLOWERING CLEMATIS

Here I propose to describe the two great groups of hardy clematis that flower early in the year: the montanas, and the atragenes. Everyone must know *Clematis montana*, a climber with enough vigour to fill a sizeable tree, decked with hundreds of small white or pale pink flowers in spring. The atragenes are very different in style, much smaller in growth and with nodding lanterns, usually blue, sometimes dusky pink or white. They comprise two wild species: *Clematis alpina*, and *C. macropetala*, which has fuller, almost double flowers. Both the montanas and the atragenes, being early-flowering, are pruned as Group 1.

Although they can be grown on a wall, the charming informality of both these groups of clematis seems to fit them better for more relaxed ways of growing: in host trees and shrubs especially. A white *C. montana* cascading down from the heights of a dark pine is one of the great sights of spring. Less successful is the combination of a montana, pink or white, in an old apple tree: they both flower at much the same time and neither gains from it. But any tree which is rather dull in late spring, and is large enough to take the weight of a full-grown montana, could be beautified by hosting one.

However, the montanas are so easy-going that they should also be the first choice if you have a high shady wall where nothing much will grow. They are perfectly capable of growing up to 12 m (40 ft). You will need to watch that they do not invade the roof tiles and gutter, however.

The atragenes

The dainty atragenes can be used in many pretty combinations. The blues combine delightfully with lime-yellow foliage (nurserymen's 'golden') such as that of *Choisya ternata* 'Sundance' or *Philadelphus coronarius* 'Aureus'. Blue or white look well with Japanese quinces in orange and flame and scarlet. The pink form of *Clematis macropetala* blends prettily with *Akebia quinata*'s dusky maroon flowers, and the planting of blue and pink *C. macropetala* together in an Ali Baba jar, as at Sissinghurst Castle in Kent, southern England, is one that anybody with a square metre to spare for such a container could emulate.

C. alpina is the European species that, in the Alps, can be found scrambling over rocks or low shrubs in open woodland, which suggests ways to grow it in the garden. The nodding, blue, lantern-like flowers appear in spring, on growth up to 2–3 m (6–10 ft). *C. alpina sibirica* is a wild form from northern Europe and Siberia, with white flowers. A selection of this called 'White Moth' is the best, with full flowers a month later than most of this group.

C. alpina is also available in several garden varieties. The largest in flower is 'Frances Rivis', its mid-blue lanterns with white stamens. 'Pamela Jackman', in deep rich blue, has broad sepals making an ample flower. A more recent variety is 'Helsingborg', a deep purple-blue with dark centre, bearing a few flowers in autumn. A paler blue is 'Columbine', with very long pointed sepals. It has an albino counterpart in 'White Columbine'. 'Burford White' is very free and early with its well-shaped white flowers against fresh pale foliage.

There are also pink varieties, of the usual rather mauve-tinted tones common in clematis. 'Ruby' has abundant dusky purple-pink flowers, and bears odd blooms during summer. The newer 'Willy' is a pale dusty pink with deeper base to the sepals and white stamens.

The Chinese *C. macropetala* has fuller flowers than *C. alpina*, usually in shades of blue, followed by silky wig-like seed heads. Named forms are worth choosing to be sure of a good colour: 'Blue Lagoon', or the somewhat larger 'Blue Bird', with deeper blue flowers. 'Maidwell Hall' is an older selection. Again, the pinks are in fact dusty, rosy mauve. As well as the old 'Markham's Pink', there is also newer 'Rosie O'Grady' in deep pink. 'White Swan' is followed by 'Snowbird', which opens its white flowers slightly later.

The montanas

The Himalayan *C. montana* flowers in the month following the atragenes but before the first of the large-flowered clematis. Pruning, if needed, is as for Group 1. Since this clematis makes vigorous growth to 6–9 m (20–30 ft) or more, it may have to be restrained to keep within bounds.

This species is naturally white, but it has a wild pink form in *C. montana rubens*, varying from rosy mauve to a washy tint, with dark foliage. Some are scented. Another natural variant is *C. montana sericea* (also listed as *C. chrysocoma sericea* or a 'Spooneri'). It has broad downy foliage and white, scentless flowers, large for this group. Flowering a month later than the other montanas is *C. montana wilsonii*, with white, chocolate-scented flowers.

When choosing a garden variety, it is worth selecting for fragrance as well as colour. 'Odorata' in very pale pink has a sweet scent, as does 'Alexander', with large, rounded, ivory-white, vanilla-scented flowers. The well-known 'Elizabeth' is pale pink, with good-sized flowers, but fades to white if grown in shade; it too is vanilla-scented. 'Pink Perfection' is similar to 'Elizabeth' in slightly deeper pink.

Pink montanas tend to have bronzed foliage. 'Picton's Variety' is one of the deepest pinks (paler in shade), less vigorous than some, and with little scent. 'Freda' is another deep pink, with bronzed foliage, while 'Rubens Superba' is a selected form of *C. m. rubens* with good dark foliage. The flower size of 'Tetrarose',

in deep rosy mauve, is the result of colchicine treatment, making this a rather coarse form. A very pretty pink is 'Marjorie', in creamy-pink with extra sepals giving a double effect, and deeper pink stamens. If you just want a stunning effect from plenty of bold white flowers, choose 'Grandiflora'.

C. chrysocoma has been mentioned several times. The true species is rather tender, with pure white flowers and golden downy foliage on non-climbing growth. A climbing hybrid with soft pink flowers is often sold under this name. Another hybrid, between *C. chrysocoma* and *C. montana rubens*, is *C.* × *vedrariensis*, with greater vigour and abundant, sizeable pink flowers among bronze-green foliage. 'Highdown' is a fine selection.

THE LANTERN-FLOWERED AND COWSLIP-FLOWERED CLEMATIS

By 'lantern-flowered', I mean the late-flowering wild clematis and their garden forms with yellow, thick-petalled flowers, often with incurving tips: Chinese lanterns, not the flared outline of the atragenes. All, and the other late-flowering varieties to be described here, flower on young wood, so are pruned as for Group 3, hard back in late winter. Alternatively you can leave them unpruned to grow as they would in the wild, when they will start to flower earlier but look messy in winter. All can reach 4.5 m (15 ft) or more.

Orange peel clematis

First is the yellow clematis often called the 'orange peel clematis'. They have finely cut foliage and thick petals, whence the nickname. In some, silky 'wigs' follow the flowers. Their bright colouring looks well among dark green or silver foliage. Less vigorous than the montanas, they can be grown through medium-sized trees that could not cope with a montana. If you can be sure of pruning them each winter, you could even grow them through shrubs. Their bright yellow flowers contrast well with the orange-red, long hips of *Rosa moyesii*, for example.

The familiar names in this group are *C. tangutica* and *C. orientalis*. The first is a rampant Chinese species with nodding yellow lanterns; it flowers long, so the later flowers are mingled with the fluffy seed heads from the first. A wild form is called *C. tangutica obtusiuscula* and has smaller, more bell-like flowers on long stalks. 'Gravetye Variety' is similar with deeper yellow bells.

C. orientalis is perhaps no longer a valid name, but I retain it as many catalogues still list it and its varieties by this name. Widely distributed throughout Asia, it is a variable species of 'orange-peel' type. L & S 13342 is a handsome, wild-collected form with very ferny foliage and thick-textured yellow lanterns, more the colour of lemon than of orange peel. 'Sherriffii' is probably synonymous. Garden varieties include 'Bill Mackenzie', with the largest flowers of all, long and well-shaped, of

Opposite: *The mother of pearl colouring of* Clematis *'Huldine' is in harmony with this soft-toned group of shrubs that includes* Cestrum parqui *and silvery foliage. The small-flowered clematis that derive from* C. viticella *range from white to deepest crimson; the wine-reds and purples are stunning among silvery foliage.*

deep yellow, followed by silky seed heads. 'Burford Variety' is probably a cross, and is very vigorous, even coarse, with stubby yellow lanterns in abundance. 'Aureolin' has rich yellow lanterns, and 'Corry' bears paler yellow flowers, a very pretty colour. Beware of 'Orange Peel', used as a variety name as well as, loosely, for the whole group. It is safer not to buy 'blind', therefore.

C. tibetana bears nodding, lemon yellow flowers with recurving tips, and glaucous foliage. Its wild variety *vernayi* is said to be what we have been calling *C. orientalis*. Bluish foliage also belongs to *C. intricata* (*C. glauca*), which has bright yellow lanterns. To some extent the odd one out, *C. serratifolia* has very pretty pale yellow lanterns with purple stamens, abundant over a shortish season, and lemon scented. Silky 'old man's beard' seed heads follow.

Cowslip-flowered clematis

Though also yellow, these are very distinct from the orange peel types. The most familiar is *C. rehderiana*, a rampant grower to 8 m (25 ft), with hairy leaves and masses of buff-primrose flowers in sprays, deliciously cowslip-scented. Progressively more restrained in growth are *C. connata*, a Himalayan species with small, primrose yellow bells in sprays, growing to 6 m (20 ft) or more; and *C. buchananiana*, with hairy foliage and small pale primrose bells on 4.5 m (15 ft) stems. Daintiest of all is *C. aethusifolia*, which has small pale yellow, jasmine-scented bells among very finely cut, grey-green foliage, and grows to around 1.5 m (5 ft).

THE VITICELLAS AND OTHER SUMMER-FLOWERING CLEMATIS

Here we find some of the most satisfactory of all garden clematis. The viticellas come in a range of colours from white to deepest velvety purple. They flower in summer with smaller flowers than the large-flowered hybrids, but very abundant. They are healthy and resistant to disease. They derive from a southern European species called *C. viticella*, almost certainly mingled with the blood of other wild clematis. Flowering in summer, they are pruned as for Group 3. This makes them ideal as companions for shrubs, through whose host branches they climb; the winter pruning frees the shrub of clematis stems so it never risks becoming cluttered. They can also be grown — as can most clematis — horizontally, over ground-covering shrubs.

The wild form of *C. viticella* is seldom seen, which is a pity, for it is very engaging, with wide nodding bells of deep purple-violet on long stalks, in summer. It can grow to 6 m (20 ft). The garden varieties, with flowers that usually look at you instead of nodding, include wine-red, white, violet, lilac, and some enchanting bicolors.

Among the reds, 'Abundance' is well named for the freedom with which it bears its light wine-red blooms on 3 m (10 ft) growth. 'Kermesina' ('Rubra'), in deeper claret, is no less free-flowering, and taller at 4.5 m (15 ft). The starry, rosy red flowers of 'Margot Koster' are borne in abundance on modest growth of 2 m (6 ft). 'Madame Julia Correvon' is valued for her beautifully poised wine-red flowers with twisted sepals, ivory-green stamens. She is a little taller, at 2.5 m (8 ft). Deepest of the reds is 'Royal Velours' in very deep velvety purple, a strong grower to 4.5 m (15 ft).

'Alba Luxurians', in white with green tips, or occasionally wholly white or wholly green, has seductively twisted sepals and is another vigorous variety reaching 4.5 m (15 ft). You should allow much the same for 'Huldine', which has pearly white, medium-sized flowers, backed with pale mauve, which last from summer to autumn.

The deep purple 'Polish Spirit', with flowers large for this group, is more restrained at 2.5 m (8 ft). There is a touch more violet in the colouring of 'Etoile Violette', its well-shaped blooms enhanced by cream stamens. It grows to 3 m (10 ft) or so.

'Betty Corning' displays pale lilac bells with recurved tips, large for this group, on growth up to 2.5 m (8 ft); while 'Pagoda' is said to be a cross between *C. viticella* and 'Etoile Rose', and has dainty flowers with narrow recurved petals of pinky mauve with a faint bar. It makes vigorous growth to 3 m (10 ft).

The bicolors range from 'Little Nell', in white margined with mauve, very pretty, through the slightly brighter 'Minuet' in which the margins are light purple, to 'Venosa Violacea', of similar colouring to 'Minuet', with red-purple veining, and boat-shaped sepals. 'Little Nell' and 'Minuet' grow to 3 m (10 ft) or so, 'Venosa Violacea' to 2.5 m (8 ft).

There are two beautiful doubles in this group. The better known is 'Purpurea Plena Elegans', a soft dusty lilac-purple double with full neat rosette flowers, growing strongly to 4.5 m (15 ft). 'Mary Rose' is a scarce but beautiful violet-blue double with silvery reverse, that seems to be much less tall in growth.

More of a collector's piece, *C. campaniflora* is closely related to *C. viticella*, and is a charming plant with wide, nodding, skimmed-milk white bells faintly flushed with mauve, in summer. Although the flowers seem so dainty this is a vigorous plant reaching 4 m (13 ft).

The traveller's joy and other late summer clematis

One of the most familiar wild clematis in Europe is *C. vitalba*, the old man's beard or traveller's joy. It is not suitable for small gardens, being very rampant and hardly noticeable in flower. A related species from southern Europe which is well worth garden space is *C. flammula*. Dark green, glossy leaves form the backdrop for masses of tiny, pure white, starry, fragrant flowers in late summer and autumn. It can easily reach 6 m (20 ft).

A cross between *C. flammula* and *C. viticella*, *C.* × *triternata* 'Rubromarginata' has cross-shaped flowers, larger than those of *C. flammula*, white with red-purple margins, very freely borne in autumn on growth to 4.5 m (15 ft). *C. potaninii* var. *souliei* (*C. fargesii* var. *souliei*) is a Chinese species with white flowers rather like an anemone's, all summer and early autumn, growing strongly to 6 m (20 ft).

Quite different from other climbing kinds, *C.* × *jouiniana* is a cross between the hyacinth-flowered herbaceous clematis and *C. vitalba*. The result is a non-clinging scrambler which will make growths up to 3 m (10 ft), vertically if you help it with

Few can resist the full, double, jade-green and white blooms of Clematis florida 'Flore Pleno'. Not the easiest of clematis, it needs a sheltered site, as here where it grows in the angle of two walls with shrubs such as Ceanothus that also appreciate protection from icy winds.

75

supports and ties, or horizontally as sprawling ground-cover. The flowers are a little like pale, milky lavender hyacinths and are borne in great masses in summer. 'Praecox' starts to flower earlier and has a very long season.

THE TEXANS

This is a group of semi-herbaceous climbing clematis derived from *C. texensis*, a species which at its best has pure red flowers. Some of this purity of colour has passed to its offspring, together with, in some, an almost tulip-shaped flower. Pruning, if needed, is as for Group 3. The Texan hybrids, all desirable, grow to between 2 and 3 m (6 to 10 ft), and include 'Duchess of Albany', with long bells of almost true pink, held upright like lily-flowered tulips, and 'Sir Trevor Lawrence' in bright cherry crimson, shaped like 'Duchess of Albany'. 'Gravetye Beauty' has ruby red bells that expand to wide stars, and 'Etoile Rose' bears its nodding open bells of deep cherry red margined with silvery pink over a three-month summer season.

There are some uncommon related species with urn-shaped flowers: *C. crispa*, with pale blue-purple bells on slender growth to 2.5 m (8 ft); the 2 m (6 ft) *C. pitcheri*, which has ribbed silver sepals with recurved tips, the interior of the flower purple with cream stamens; and *C. viorna*, a herbaceous species that may reach 2 m (6 ft) each season, bearing small pitcher-shaped flowers formed of thick red-brown sepals, yellow within.

FOR CONSERVATORIES AND SHELTERED WALLS

Lastly, a mixed bunch of clematis which have in common that, in the colder parts of the world at least, they need a warm sheltered wall or even conservatory treatment. Between them, they span the seasons, with some flowering even in winter.

Grown outside, *C. cirrhosa* flowers during spells of open winter weather. It is evergreen, with divided leaves, bronzed in winter, and nodding pale green-primrose flowers, freckled with red-brown within. The fresh lemon scent is only noticeable under glass. Its variety *balearica* has even more finely cut leaves. 'Freckles' is heavily marked within with maroon-pink, while 'Wisley Form' is an unspotted creamy primrose. They can be treated as Group 1, or can be hard-pruned yearly immediately after flowering. Unpruned, they grow to 4 m (13 ft).

Another winter-flowering species is *C. napaulensis*. Winter-green and summer-deciduous, it bears creamy bells with bright purple protruding stamens. Height and pruning treatment are the same as for *C. cirrhosa*. *C. afoliata* is a curiosity, virtually leafless, looking more like a rush than a clematis, with straw-yellow flowers, said to be daphne-scented, in winter (or early spring if grown outdoors). Group 1 treatment again applies, but this is a modest plant reaching only 2 m.

The star of the spring season is *C. armandii*. Bold, polished evergreen leaves of narrow oblong outline set off abundant flowers with strong vanilla perfume. To be sure of good flowers, buy a named form: 'Apple Blossom', white with blush pink, or 'Snowdrift', pure white. It is fairly hardy, but the foliage can be spoiled in cold winters. The young leaves are attractively bronzed. Best if pruned each year after flowering to keep it tidy, *C. armandii* can easily reach 9 m (30 ft).

C. forsteri is more modest, but very charming when massed with fresh yellow-green flowers, lemon scented, in spring. It should reach 3 m (10 ft). It is from New Zealand, like the handsome *C. paniculata*. Flowering in spring, this evergreen species looks rather like a superb, pure white *C. montana* to the casual glance, but is less rampant at 3 m (10 ft).

In summer it is the turn of *C. florida*. Slightly tricky, needing protection, this is cherished for two exquisite varieties that survive. 'Flore Pleno' is a double, with a full central rosette of green-washed white surrounded by six white guard sepals. 'Sieboldii' has the same white guard sepals but the centre is a rosette of bright purple with paler flecks, recalling a passion flower. Both should have Group 2 treatment. They grow to 2.5 m (8 ft).

By the time autumn comes round again, *C. terniflora* (*C. maximowicziana*) is in flower. It needs a good summer baking to flower freely, and is better in continental climates than maritime. The abundant white, starry flowers are scented like *C. flammula*. It grows to about 6 m (20 ft).

7
FRAGRANT CLIMBERS

FRAGRANCE, MORE THAN ANY other stimulant of our five senses, has the ability to evoke memories. Often, it is no more than a fleeting impression, so brief that all we retain is a tantalizing impression of nostalgia or poignance. Then again, a fragrance may bring back a flood of memories that we thought lost. This extraordinary ability gives it a special place in our hearts. Certain climbers, as we have seen, have the quality of fragrance in abundance.

This, as much as their beauty, is why honeysuckles and jasmines, wisteria and sweet peas, are cherished. The mystery is that other, no less sweetly scented climbers are scarcely known.

HONEYSUCKLES

Honeysuckles belong to the genus *Lonicera*. Unlike roses and clematis, many of those we grow are the wild species, or garden forms very close to them. I have to tell you, however, that the most showy honeysuckles, those with the brightest flowers, lack scent. This lapse will be noted wherever appropriate.

Most honeysuckles do best with their roots cool and shaded, and their heads in dappled shade or sun, emulating their native woodland margins. Some need full sun; a few do best in full shade and will even bring colour to dark corners. All the climbing kinds have twining stems, and in some vigorous species this can be a problem, as host plants become choked and strangled. Honeysuckles are increased by cuttings in summer or autumn.

Favourite fragrant honeysuckles

The common honeysuckle or woodbine of European woodland edges, copses and hedgerows is *Lonicera periclymenum*. It is distinguished from *L. caprifolium*, a wide-spread species found in Asia as well as Europe, by the uppermost leaves, which are not joined. The flowers of the woodbine are both striking and delectably perfumed, carrying far on the air especially at dusk and dawn. They open in

Opposite: *The perennial pea,* Lathyrus latifolius, *is a herbaceous climber that can be trained to fill the gap in a border where earlier flowers such as oriental poppies have gone over. Grown as spreading ground cover, as here among greyish gravel, it is ideal for a low-maintenance garden. Just shear off the herbaceous stems in winter, and the plant will grow again in spring.*

summer. Best in semi-shade, this honeysuckle grows vigorously to 6 m (20 ft). Garden varieties include 'Belgica', the early Dutch honeysuckle, of bushy growth with flowers madder purple in bud, fading to pink, yellow within; and 'Serotina', the late Dutch honeysuckle, with flowers dark purple on the outside and pinkish within, flowering until autumn. 'Graham Thomas' is a fine newer variety with large, fragrant, cream flowers.

L. caprifolium is characterized by the upper two or three pairs of leaves being connate, that is, joined together in cupped form at the base, around the stem. In the uppermost cup sits a cluster of white to deep cream flowers. These are sometimes, as in 'Pauciflora', suffused with pink. They open in early summer and are deliciously fragrant. The early cream or perfoliate honeysuckle, as it is also called, is a strong grower to 8 m (25 ft).

One of the most popular in gardens is *Lonicera × americana,* a cross between *L. caprifolium* and the Mediterranean *L. etrusca,* resulting in a vigorous climber to 9 m (30 ft). It bears fragrant white flowers in summer which age through ivory and primrose to deep yellow. The outside of the flower is often purple-flushed, especially in full sun.

L. etrusca itself is semi-evergreen in mild districts, bearing glaucous foliage and fragrant cream flowers aging to yellow, tinged with red-purple, in summer. The selection 'Superba' has very large clusters of flower. At 4 m (13 ft), it is more restrained in growth. One of the most suitable for small gardens is *L. × heckrottii* 'Gold Flame'. The brightest of the fragrant honeysuckles, with blood of *L. × americana* for scent and *L. sempervirens* for colour, it has flowers of yellow and orange-pink, opening from mid to late summer on rather shrubby growth to 3 m (10 ft). It is best in light shade.

By contrast, *L. splendida,* a Spanish species with beautiful, bright glaucous-blue foliage, needs full sun. The fragrant flowers are red-purple, yellowish within, and are borne in summer. Where suited it will grow to 6 m (20 ft).

The evergreen honeysuckles

The most familiar of the evergreen, fragrant honeysuckles is *L. japonica.* The Japanese honeysuckle is vigorous and easy, with evergreen foliage and powerfully fragrant white flowers aging through cream to primrose and buff, borne over a long summer season. Ideal for fences and large tree stumps, it is not so good for house walls. 'Halliana' is a fine form, while variety *repens* has purple-flushed flowers. These grow to 10 m. The more compact 'Aureoreticulata' hardly flowers unless in full, baking sun, but is valued for its gold-netted foliage.

L. giraldii, with small but abundant scented flowers, red-purple outside and yellow within in summer, amid dense growth of softly hairy, evergreen foliage, is evergreen. So also is *L. henryi,* which makes leafy growth to 10 m (33 ft), with small yellow flowers, flushed maroon-purple, in summer. Both make luxuriant cover. The first is slightly tender, and grows to 6 m (20 ft).

Showy but scentless

The trumpet honeysuckle from the eastern United States, *L. sempervirens,* is a vigorous evergreen with leaves bluish beneath. The tubular, bright scarlet flowers are borne in whorls in summer. 'Sulphurea' has yellow flowers. Both need some shelter, when they will grow to 6 m (20 ft). A better choice for a small garden might be *L. × brownii*. Bright and scentless, this has its vivid scarlet or coral colouring from *L. sempervirens*. The foliage is bluish. Two forms are offered: 'Dropmore Scarlet', which has a very long season, and 'Fuchsioides' (fuchsia-like).

L. × tellmanniana is another hybrid of *L. sempervirens,* this time with *L. tragophylla.* It bears its bright coppery-yellow, long trumpets in clusters from early to high summer, and is scentless but spectacular. Part shade is best. Both this and its parent may grow to 6 m (20 ft). *L. tragophylla,* a Chinese honeysuckle, is even more beautiful than the last, with long, large, scentless trumpets of rich yellow, in summer. It does best in part or full shade.

JASMINE

The jasmines are a tropical and subtropical genus, so that the few we can grow in cooler climes are just a fraction of the many different wild species. Given their origins, it is not surprising that jasmines need a sunny position; but they do not like to be too dry at the root. They are scramblers or twiners; all have the characteristic propellor-shaped flower. They can be propagated by cuttings, taken in summer or autumm.

The very name comes from the Arabic *yasmin.* In Arab countries jasmines can be found wreathing garden fences, filling the air with their fragrance especially at dawn and dusk. The essential oil which contains the perfume is much used, as attar or in more sophisticated creations.

When that heady perfume assails our noses, therefore, we may legitimately imagine warm Mediterranean or Levantine nights, or even think of the fragrant garlands that are so popular in the Indian subcontinent and elsewhere. At the same time, the summer jasmine, *Jasminum officinale,* is an old cottage favourite with much homelier associations of fragrant bowers and flower-wreathed porches. It owes its popularity to its vigorous growth and abundant, very sweetly scented white flowers. It is a true twining climber reaching 9 m (30 ft) when suited. Several forms are available. *J. officinale affine* has larger flowers suffused with pink on the outside. Two have variegated foliage: 'Argenteovariegatum' with leaves marked with creamy white, and the very showy 'Aureum' with gold-splashed leaves; the stems, too, are often yellow and green.

J. beesianum is the only jasmine with red flowers — in fact, they are velvety red to carmine, and slightly fragrant, opening in early summer. It is a Chinese species and hardy. In sun it is more or less bushy; in light shade it will climb to 2 m (6 ft) or so. Its hybrid with the summer jasmine is *J. × stephanense.* The result is a vigorous, pink-flowered twining climber reaching 7.5 m (25 ft), marred only by its tendency to show white-mottled leaves which give it a rather unhealthy appearance.

The tender white jasmines

If your climate permits, you should certainly grow one of the more tender jasmines. *J. polyanthum* is related to the summer jasmine but less hardy, and is

The long, elegant trumpets of Lonicera tragophylla *lack only fragrance. A shaded wall suits this Chinese honeysuckle well, and grey stone is the ideal backdrop for its clear butter yellow colouring.*

Opposite: *Wisteria is first choice for a pergola, for the hanging tresses are borne close to the eye and nose. This is* Wisteria floribunda *'Multijuga', which has the longest racemes of all, often as much as 90 cm (3 ft) long. The less spectacular* W. sinensis, *however, has a sweeter fragrance.*

often grown as a house plant in cold areas, when it needs severe pruning to keep it under control. Indoors its heavy swooning perfume is enough to fill a whole room; the flowers open in late winter. Outside it needs a warm sheltered position, and will start to flower in spring, often continuing until autumn. The flowers are white, tinted with pink or crimson in bud, and are borne in large clusters. It can easily grow to 3 m (10 ft) or more.

Others are more tender still, such as *Jasminum angulare,* a South African species. The deliciously fragrant white flowers in late summer are set off by dark evergreen foliage. It is semi-twining and need support, reaching 3 m (10 ft). The Madeiran *J. azoricum* also needs protection from the cold. Perfumed white flowers open from purple-flushed buds, their season lasting from summer into winter. It is more of a twiner than the last, growing to 4 m, and has slightly smaller flowers.

A cosmopolitan genus, jasmines are also found in the Antipodes. *J. simplicifolium suavissimum* is an Australian species with fragrant white, pink-flushed flowers in late summer, distinguished by its very narrow leaves. It needs conservatory protection in cold climates. Of all the white jasmines, though, the finest for warm gardens or conservatories is *J. sambac.* The wonderfully fragrant, large-flowered white jasmine from India is too tender to grow outside in

cold gardens, but is superb where the winters are mild. Its evergreen, glossy leaves are unlobed, whereas most jasmines have leaves of from three to many leaflets. The flowers blush pink as they age and are borne almost without pause in warm climates. 'Grand Duke' is a double-flowered form, growing to 3 m (10 ft) or more.

The yellow jasmines

Although the winter jasmine, *J. nudiflorum,* is not really a climber at all, but a sprawling shrub, it is too well known and too often grown as a wall plant in cold climates, to be left out. Cheering yellow flowers are borne in winter. The young stems and the leaves are rich green (there is also a yellow-leaved form 'Aureum'). It will grow and flower almost anywhere, even on a sunless wall. If trained upwards it can reach 3 m (10 ft) or more.

The primrose jasmine, *J. mesnyi (J. primulinum),* is a slightly tender Chinese climber with larger, clear yellow flowers, sometimes semi-double with up to ten petals, in spring and early summer. The leaves, which are retained in mild winters, are deep green. It will succeed outside in warm gardens, but in areas with cold climates it needs conservatory protection. It can grow to 3 m (10 ft).

J. floridum, another yellow-flowered jasmine, is more of a scrambler up to 2.5 m (8 ft), evergreen or semi-evergreen, with small but very abundant flowers throughout summer. It needs a sheltered spot in full sun.

FRAGRANT FAVOURITES: WISTERIA AND SWEET PEAS

Wisteria

The wisteria's long tresses of lavender-mauve pea-flowers and its sweet bean-field fragrance earn it a place alongside honeysuckle and jasmine as a favourite garden climber. All the wisterias are twining climbers, most of them extremely vigorous. They thrive in any ordinary soil but need full sun to flower well. In Italy, for example, they put up a spectacular display in many a courtyard, often following on from the primrose jasmine.

In the early years after planting, it is quite usual for all their energies to go into making growth, leaving nothing over for flowers. During this stage the shoots should be tied to the structure they are intended to cover — the wires you have fixed to a wall, the uprights and cross-beams of a pergola, the branches of a host tree. There may be too many shoots, so that you need to thin out, removing some to encourage the others to grow stout and strong. Remaining laterals (side shoots) should be pruned in summer, shortening them to about 15 cm (6 in), and again in winter, when you cut them back to only two or three buds.

This regime of pruning, which continues through the life of the plant, will encourage flowering spurs. Never give a wisteria a nitrogen-rich fertilizer, which will simply promote more leafy growth at the expense of flowers. Sometimes, a restricted root run will encourage more flowers.

Whether you grow your wisteria on a wall or on a free-standing structure, remember that the long tresses of flower should be able to hang free. I recall a large country house in England's West Country where *W. floribunda* 'Multijuga' had been trained to the eaves and around the windows, so carefully that each arm-long trail of flower hung clear. Elsewhere, this wisteria has been grown along a wooden bridge spanning a stream. Over still water you have a double effect, the flowers reflected in the pool below. Wisterias are also ideal for pergolas as their hanging flowers ensure that you, not the sky above, get the benefit of the blooms.

Propagation is by layering, or by cuttings taken in late summer. These are not always easy, but rooting can be encouraged if the cuttings are given bottom heat.

The choice in wisterias

Despite their beauty and appeal, wisterias have never been extensively bred like roses or clematis. However, there is a wide enough choice for all but the most vast of gardens. This is especially true of *W. floribunda*. The Japanese wisteria has clockwise-twining stems and bears its fragrant, lavender-violet flowers in slender trails, in early summer. It is a vigorous plant and easily reaches 9 m (30 ft) in height. It also comes in white: 'Alba' has white flowers, sometimes with a hint of lilac, in racemes up to 60 cm (2 ft) long. 'Snow Showers' is a fine, more recent white variety.

'Multijuga' ('Macrobotrys') has the longest racemes of all, 60–90 cm (2–3 ft) long. Tresses up to 1.8 m (6 ft) have been recorded. The individual flowers are of the usual colour, the standard mauve, the keel blue-violet. By contrast, 'Issai' has rather shorter tresses than usual, of lilac-blue flowers. Some say it is a hybrid with *W. sinensis*. 'Violacea Plena' has double lilac flowers.

Pink is a more unexpected colour in wisterias, but there are for all that several to choose from. One of the first to be introduced was 'Rosea', which gives a pink effect, the standards pale pink and the keel violet. The racemes are quite long. Cleaner colouring belongs to 'Pink Ice'; while 'Peaches and Cream' has pink buds opening to white flowers.

W. sinensis, the Chinese wisteria, is easily distinguished from the Japanese, because its stems twine anti-clockwise. It is even more vigorous, growing as much as 30 m (100 ft) and able to fill a tall tree. It is more fragrant than the Japanese, and the mauve or lilac flowers open virtually all at once in spring, with the unfurling leaves. It will often bear a small second crop of bloom in late summer. 'Alba', with white flowers, is especially sweetly scented.

Some people complain that their wisterias refuse to flower. Sometimes this may be due to immaturity. 'Prematura' and 'Prematura Alba', lilac and white respectively, are varieties said to flower from an early age. 'Prolific', as its name suggests, flowers very freely; the racemes are longer than usual.

Double varieties are known: 'Plena' has double lilac flowers, and 'Black Dragon' has double flowers of deep purple.

Wisteria 'Caroline' is probably a hybrid. Quite a new variety, it promises very well with its deep blue-purple, very fragrant flowers.

W. venusta is a beautiful, though scarcely scented, wisteria introduced from

Japanese gardens, with ivory-white flowers in abundant short racemes in early summer. The individual flowers are large, and last long in beauty. It grows to about 9 m (30 ft).

Sweet peas and their relatives

From the references to keels and standards and pea-flowers, you will gather that sweet peas are in the same family as wisteria. As their name suggests, their fragrance is their special and precious characteristic. How sad that plant breeders, in their search for bigger and brighter flowers, have so often forgotten the 'sweet' and concentrated on other attributes.

All the climbing peas, whether annual or perennial, scented or not, are easy to grow from seed, as described in the chapter on propagation. The perennials can also be grown from basal cuttings. The perennial species can be grown in almost all the ways other climbers can be grown. Some are excellent for filling gaps in flower borders; once an early-flowering plant such as the oriental poppy is over, the flexible stems of the pea can be trained forwards to hide the empty space. They can be grown on fences and through shrubs, on trellis or tumbling down a bank. *Climbing* sweet peas need the support of fine pea sticks or of canes if you do not offer them a convenient shrub. They attach themselves by tendrils at the ends of the leaves.

If you want fragrance above all, go for the old-fashioned varieties of sweet pea, or pick carefully from the catalogues the varieties that are specifically marked 'very fragrant'. As there are so many different sweet peas, and more are introduced each year, I propose here to mention only some of the old varieties that are worth preserving.

L. odoratus, as its name suggests, is the original sweet pea. In its wild form from Italy and Sicily it is an annual climber growing up to 2 m (6 ft), with fragrant, purple flowers. Old varieties such as 'Matucana' and 'Quito', which have magenta and purple flowers, or 'Painted Lady', which dates from the 18th century, in rose-pink and white, are also intensely perfumed. Nineteenth-century sweet peas were developed by Henry Eckford, who created the 'Grandiflora' range; but by 1914 they had been superseded by the Spencer sweet peas from the firm of Unwin. These were the first to bear frilled blooms, in the pale pink varieties 'Countess Spencer' and 'Gladys Unwin'. A few of Henry Eckford's varieties survive, and some of the early Spencers. Among newer varieties, it seems almost a rule of thumb that the brighter the colour, the less the fragrance.

There are also other kinds of *Lathyrus,* lacking fragrance but many, nonetheless, too beautiful to ignore. *Lathyrus grandiflorus* is a perennial from southern Europe known as the everlasting pea, a familiar old garden plant with spreading, tuberous roots, herbaceous stems up to 1.5 m (5 ft) long, and large flowers in twos and threes over a long summer season. The standards are magenta-violet, the wings

Opposite: *The cupped flowers of* Akebia quinata *open in spring among bronzed green foliage. It is a vigorous twining climber, valued for its spicy vanilla fragrance and unusual chocolate-maroon colouring.*

purple and the keel is maroon-pink. The name everlasting pea is also sometimes given to *L. latifolius,* the perennial pea, another European plant, one of the finest for growing among shrubs, down banks, or as a border filler. The herbaceous stems are up to 2 m (6 ft) long. The large, scentless flowers borne in racemes of up to fifteen blooms. Typically, they are magenta-pink; there is an exquisite white form, *L.l. albus* or 'White Pearl', and clear pinks such as 'Pink Pearl'.

L. tuberosus is a European pea rather like a smaller version of *L. latifolius,* with pink flowers in summer and herbaceous stems up to 1.5 m (5 ft). The Persian everlasting pea, *L. rotundifolius,* has flowers of a pretty and unusual shade of pink with coppery and terracotta undertones, borne in summer. The leaves are fresh green, and the herbaceous stems grow to 2 m (6 ft) each year.

Blue, as always, seems to have an allure other colours do not. *L. nervosus (L. magellanicus)* is Lord Anson's blue pea, almost unobtainable for many years but now back in cultivation, and deservedly so, for it is both fragrant and beautiful. The clear periwinkle blue flowers are borne many together in racemes during summer. The grey-green foliage adds to a gentle colour scheme. The herbaceous stems grow to 1.5 m (5 ft). The annual *L. sativus* is not so distinguished, but very pretty, with flowers of clear turquoise blue, on 1.2 m (4 ft) stems. *L. sativus* is sometimes offered under names such as *azureus* or *caeruleus.*

UNUSUAL FRAGRANT CLIMBERS

Jasmines, honeysuckle and roses are justifiably among the most popular climbers because of their fragrance as much as their beauty. They are not, however, the only climbers with scented flowers. It would be a pity if they were allowed to overshadow less familiar but no less worthy plants.

The climbers I want to describe in this section are a varied collection, and I shall therefore suggest ways to use them as I describe them, rather than putting forward general ideas as with the more homogeneous groups. Elsewhere in the book, other climbers with fragrant flowers will also appear, if their other attributes seem to me to be more important in the garden.

Akebia quinata is a Far Eastern climber with cupped, chocolate-maroon flowers in drooping sprays in spring. They have a spicy vanilla fragrance, and their colour would be enhanced by the soft dusty pink of *Clematis macropetala* 'Markham's Pink'. The dark green foliage is attractive, each leaf composed of five rounded leaflets. After hot summers, purplish, sausage-shaped fruits may form. The vigorous twining stems grow to 9 m (30 ft) or more. Increase by layering, or take hardwood or semi-ripe cuttings. *A. trifoliata* is similar but less common; it is distinguished by having only three leaflets. A hybrid between the two is *A. ×pentaphylla.* All the akebias can be used on pergolas, fences, walls, or among large shrubs or small trees.

Related to the akebias are the holboellias, evergreen, twining climbers from Asia, with separate male and female flowers; but it must be said neither is showy. They are suitable for either sun or shade, but need a fairly sheltered position. *Holboellia coriacea* has purplish-white male flowers and slightly larger, greener female flowers in spring, hidden among bold, leathery foliage. The wonderfully fragrant flowers of *H. latifolia* open rather earlier than those of *H. coriacea;* male flowers are greenish and female dingy brown-purple. Otherwise it is very similar. If you have room for only one, it should be this. Either can be increased by layering, seed or cuttings; they grow to 6 m (20 ft).

Stauntonia hexaphylla, a Far Eastern climber, is very like the holboellias, with fragrant whitish-mauve flowers in spring. The twining stems are set with large, leathery, deep green foliage and may reach 9 m (30 ft). Like the holboellias it may after hot summers produce fleshy, sausage-like fruits with purple skin and edible pulp. This is said to be rather tasteless. The seeds can be sown to make new plants, or you can take late summer cuttings.

None of the true climbing hydrangeas is fragrant, but *Decumaria barbara,* a root-clinging climber related to the hydrangeas, and native of the south-eastern United States, has white, fragrant flowers opening in summer among glossy foliage, which is shed in autumn. It needs a sheltered position, and grows to 9 m (30 ft). It can be raised from late summer cuttings, as can *D. sinensis,* a Chinese species less common than the last. It is one of the few hardy, evergreen, self-clinging climbers. The honey-scented, cream flowers, like little bells, are held in nodding clusters and open in summer. It reaches 4.5 m (15 ft).

The trachelospermums are beautiful evergreen climbers with flowers like jasmine. *Trachelospermum asiaticum,* from Japan and Korea, makes dense cover up to 6 m (20 ft) with its half twining, half self-clinging stems and small glossy leaves. The creamy white flowers age to soft buff yellow and are shaped like small periwinkle flowers. They are deliciously fragrant, and open in late summer. Full sun or light shade, with shelter in cold areas, is needed. *T. jasminoides* is larger in leaf, with white flowers aging to cream and a strong sweet perfume. It has a beautiful form 'Variegatum' with the leaves marbled in cream, often turning to crimson-pink in winter. This is hardier than the plain green form. Another, distinguished as 'Wilson 776', has bronze-green leaves which turn rich red in winter. Trachelospermums are propagated by layers, or late summer cuttings.

The last two fragrant climbers included here need warm, sheltered walls, or even glasshouse protection in very cold gardens. *Dregea sinensis* (*Wattakaka sinensis*) is an unusual twining climber from China, with flowers rather like those of a hoya, white stars flecked with red. They are borne in hanging clusters of 10 to 25, in summer, and are sweetly scented. The leaves are grey-felted on the undersides. It will grow to 3 m (10 ft), and is propagated by late summer cuttings, or from seed.

Mandevilla laxa (*M. suaveolens*) is the hardiest mandevilla, but still needs a warm sheltered wall in cool gardens. Despite its common name of Chilean jasmine, it is neither a jasmine nor Chilean, but a native of Argentina related to periwinkle. A twining climber to 4.5 m (15 ft), it has pure white, delicately fragrant flowers, propellor-shaped like huge periwinkles, in summer. The narrow leaves are dark green and slightly bronzed. Long twinned seed pods follow the flowers, the shiny black seeds nestling in silky fluff. Cuttings are the best method of increase, as seedlings may be slow to flower, or bear poorly formed blooms.

8
CLIMBERS FOR FOLIAGE

AMONG THE CLIMBERS I HAVE already described there have been a few with lovely leaves. The variegated trachelospermum in the preceding chapter could earn a place among the best of foliage plants, for example. On the whole, though, flowers have held centre stage until now. It is time to meet some climbers grown more for their foliage. Just as much as any other foliage plant, they may be valued for many reasons. Perhaps they are evergreen, bringing a furnished look to the bleak winter scene. Perhaps they colour brightly in autumn. Several have variegated or coloured foliage, and a few are just plain green, but win favour because of the size, the shape, or the texture of their leaves.

EVERGREEN CLIMBERS

What every gardener would like is a self-clinging, hardy, evergreen climber with beautiful foliage and colourful, fragrant flowers. Let me tell you right away that in cool-temperate gardens there is no such thing. Cream or white flowers, yes; fragrance, sometimes; self-clinging, a few; hardy, some. But the very scarcity of these desirable attributes means that we cherish all the more the few evergreen climbers we have. Gardeners in the tropics do not realize how fortunate they are to be able to grow outside, as creepers and lianas, many of the foliage plants we treat as house-plants in these colder parts.

What do you consider to be the most important part of your garden? Of course, all gardeners have their favourite plants and their favourite corners. Objectively, though, surely the area by your front door must be one of the most important. If you have planted climbing roses or clematis or honeysuckle, they will look marvellous in their short season. At all other times of the year, you may well wish them gone. There is nothing smart about bare rose stems, winter's clematis all set with blackened, dead leaves, or a flowerless tangle of honeysuckle. This is where evergreen climbers really come into their own.

The evergreen climbing hydrangea, or one of its close relatives, would make a good choice to surround a front door facing away from the sun. However, you

Opposite: *The Boston ivy,* Parthenocissus tricuspidata *'Veitchii', is valued for its autumn colour, vivid against the grey stone of this house. A vigorous climber, it will reach great heights, concealing an ugly shed or outhouse. But remember that it will drop its leaves in winter.*

should not expect the same bright flowers as on the familiar mophead kinds in pink or blue. *Hydrangea serratifolia* comes from Chile, and bears, in late summer, a froth of creamy blossom almost completely lacking the sterile florets which are the showy part of hydrangea flowers. It is a self-clinging root climber reaching 4 m (13 ft) or more, hardy in a sheltered site. Increase by layering or by taking cuttings in late summer. Another of the climbing hydrangea tribe is *Pileostegia viburnoides*, valued for being frost-hardy, self-clinging and evergreen, growing to 6 m (20 ft). It has long, oblong, leathery, deep green leaves, and in late summer and autumn it bears wide heads of tiny ivory flowers. It is best in rich, moist soil, in shade or sun. Propagation is as for *Hydrangea serratifolia*.

The trachelospermums, already described in Chapter 7, make ideal 'front door' climbers. For something more unusual, you could choose *Berberidopsis corallina*. This is the coral plant, a Chilean evergreen with twining stems up to 3 m (10 ft), and rich green foliage rather like holly, but not so fiercely armed. The crimson flowers are held in hanging clusters and open from blood-red globular buds in summer and autumn. Give it a sheltered, half-shaded site in neutral or lime-free soil with plenty of humus. The coral plant is easily increased by cuttings, which can even be taken in autumn and winter if you can give them bottom heat. *Ercilla volubilis* is another Chilean evergreen, much less easy to obtain than the coral plant, and needing similar conditions. The self-clinging stems are set with deep green, pale-veined leaves that make an attractive, quiet pattern against a wall. It can also be trained against a tree to clothe the trunk. Little whitish bells in dense short spikes open in spring. It grows to 6 m (20 ft), but can easily be pruned to half as tall. Make more by layering the stems, or take late summer cuttings.

Handsome though they are, the evergreen members of the bramble family are not exactly front door material, but do not think they are all fiercely armed weeds, like the common bramble, even if they can be increased in the same way, by tip layering. One of the best is *Rubus henryi*, very handsome with its three-lobed leaves with dark, shining surface, on long stems. Variety *bambusarum* is elegant in leaf with its three distinct leaflets. They bear poor little pink flowers, followed by shiny blackberries, and grow to 6 m (20 ft).

R. flagelliflorus is best trained to a pillar or trellis, for it produces an abundance of scarcely prickly stems each year from the base rather like a rambler rose, reaching 3 m (10 ft). The pointed, heart-shaped leaves are buff-felted beneath, dark green and often marbled above. The white flowers and edible blackberries are of not much account. *R. ichangensis*, quite newly reintroduced from China, is not fully evergreen, but handsome in large, leathery, tapering leaf. It needs shelter, and bears good red fruits in clusters.

The last, *R. tricolor*, is a trailer, not a climber, with long 3 m (10 ft) red-furred stems, glossy, dark green, rounded leaves white beneath, and white flowers followed by red fruits. It is ideal for large-scale ground cover on banks, below trees or among large shrubs.

Many ivies make excellent cover for the ground as well as for walls and tree trunks. Because so many of the popular garden varieties have variegated foliage, I shall describe them all together, plain and coloured, later in this chapter.

CLIMBERS FOR AUTUMN COLOUR

The words 'fall colour' evoke images of scarlet and golden leaves blazing out across New England maple forests, and dropping with the frosts to carpet the ground beneath the newly bare branches of the trees. For vivid autumn foliage, climbers in the vine family are unsurpassed, and many can compete with any maple.

Most of the vines can be planted to grow into trees. This often means that their foliage, in its dying glory, can be seen against the light. A silver birch, say, filled with the scarlet glory of a Virginia creeper, its leaves haloed by the autumn sun, is a sight to treasure.

Parthenocissus is a genus of vines which includes the Virginia creeper and others no less beautiful in autumn leaf colour. Many have little adhesive pads at the end of the leaf tendrils, whereas the self-sticking pads are absent in *Ampelopsis* and *Vitis*. This makes *Parthenocissus* ideal for walls, fences, pillars and trees alike. Summer cuttings can be rooted to make new plants.

There is a simple way of remembering the difference between *Parthenocissus quinquefolia*, the true Virginia creeper, and the Boston ivy with which it is often confused. 'Quinquefolia' means with five leaves; each leaf has five leaflets. The Roman notation for five is V, the initial letter of Virginia creeper. It comes, as the name suggests, from the eastern United States. In autumn the leaves take on brilliant tints of scarlet, flame and crimson. The plant is self-clinging and has great vigour up to 12 m (40 ft) or more. *P. tricuspidata* is the Boston ivy (not, of course, a true ivy) with three leaflets (or sometimes only one), not five like the Virginia creeper. It is no less vivid in autumn in shades of crimson, and its sticky pads keep it firmly attached to its support. Its vigour makes it ideal for large, bare walls, where it can reach 18 m (60 ft) or even more. Be sure to keep it out of gutters and from beneath roof tiles. 'Veitchii' is the form originally introduced from the Far East; it has purplish young foliage.

Even more beautiful than these rampant and colourful vines is *P. henryana*, which has leaves composed of three to five leaflets, each deep velvety green flushed with bronze, picked out in pink along the veins. The best colour comes on plants grown in shade. In autumn the leaves turn to rich crimson. It makes vigorous growth to 6 m (20 ft) or more, and is best in a sheltered position.

The true vines are called *Vitis*. The common grape vine and many other ornamental vines belong here. Most are easy and vigorous, and many colour brightly in autumn. They can be grown in trees, on fences or walls, and on pergolas. Indeed, a vine is a classic cover for a pergola, giving shade and delighting the eye with its luxuriant foliage as well as the palate with its fruit. Vines appreciate a rich soil and do best in full sun. They are propagated by eye cuttings taken in winter, except for *V. coignetiae*, which is best layered to make new plants. This Japanese species, bearing very large, rounded to heart-shaped leaves which turn scarlet, orange and coppery purple in autumn, has great vigour and if allowed can reach the tops of tall trees. It also looks splendid against grey, lichen-covered stone; allow 10 m (33 ft) or more.

COLOURED FOLIAGE

There are few climbers with coloured foliage other than variegated. *Lonicera splendida* (see Chapter 7) has blue-glaucous leaves and *Araujia sericofera* (see Chapter 10) has greyish foliage, as has the dusty miller vine. As we have seen in Chapter 7, some of the trachelospermums turn red in winter, and so does *Euonymus fortunei* 'Coloratus', a vigorous, plain-leaved variety; but only the teinturier grape has leaves that are purple in summer. There are a few climbers with yellow leaves, such as the golden hop.

The dusty miller vine and the teinturier grape are both garden forms of the grape vine, *Vitis vinifera*, and are grown for their beauty rather than their fruit. They grow to 6 m (20 ft). The dusty miller vine, 'Incana', gets its name from its grey-green leaves, which are white-felted when young. The fruits are black. The teinturier grape is called 'Purpurea' on account of its purple foliage, white-downy when young. Because of the dark colouring that suffuses the whole plant the grapes are black even when unripe, so you may get an unpleasant surprise if you taste one. It is a beautiful companion for a dusky pink clematis or passion flower: the two together could cover a grey stone wall, or a gazebo.

Humulus lupulus is the common hop, well known in hopyards wherever beer is brewed. It is a very vigorous plant making a tangle of herbaceous stems up to 4.5 m (15 ft) tall. For the garden the variety to choose is 'Aureus', very colourful in fresh lime yellow. Give it a dark background if possible. To keep to the true 'Aureus', divide the plant or take basal cuttings in spring.

VARIEGATED FOLIAGE

Though climbers with coloured foliage are few, there are, on the other hand, several with variegated foliage. Some, such as *Trachelospermum jasminoides* 'Variegatum' and the 'silver' and 'golden' jasmines, have already been described, as has the golden-netted honeysuckle.

Variegated climbers need to be used with the same care as other variegated plants: too many, and the effect is fussy, the individual detail lost. Contrasted with plain green foliage, or as part of a carefully thought-out colour scheme, they can add greatly to the garden picture. They have especial value in winter, bringing brightness to a scene that might otherwise be drab. For this reason, I shall describe first a selection of evergreen, variegated climbers. The two great groups, for cooler climates, are the ivies and euonymus.

Euonymus

Variegated forms of *Eunonymus fortunei* are so often sold as ground cover that it is easy to forget how good many are as climbers. Most, if given a suitable support

Opposite: *The teinturier vine,* Vitis vinifera 'Purpurea', *shows its changing play of leaf tones from grey-bloomed purple on first emerging, through shades of plum to green. As a bonus, it bears bunches of black grapes in autumn. For extra colour, weave a dusky pink clematis through it — the double* 'Proteus' *perhaps.*

such as a wall or a tree-trunk, will climb 2.5 m (8 ft) or more, attaching themselves by stem roots. Any good soil suits them, in sun or part shade. They are increased by summer or autumn cuttings.

The brightest are those with green and gold foliage. 'Emerald 'n' Gold' is just as its name says, and apparently endlessly popular. If you grow it in full sun it will often add pink to the green and bright yellow combination, which then becomes a bit too hectic. 'Sheridan Gold' is green suffused with yellow, making a softer effect. Leaves brightly splashed with gold at the centre have given 'Sunspot' its name. 'Golden Tip' has new foliage tipped yellow, bright against the dark older foliage.

White variegations are more soothing, if less warmly cheering in winter. 'Silver Queen' is a good old variety with quite large leaves, green variegated with white. Another old kind, but still a good one, is 'Variegatus', with grey-green leaves margined white and often tinged pink. 'Emerald Gaiety' is quieter than it sounds, with green leaves variegated in creamy white.

Ivies

Although the wild ivy is of course plain green, so many of the popular house and garden varieties have variegated leaves that I include them, green and coloured, all together. In the wild, before man came along and provided ruins, churches and castles, ivy grew in trees. It may also do so in the garden, along with other ever-greens. With so many varieties to choose from, you can match the vigour of the host tree and the ivy.

The ivies can be used in many other situations as well: ground-cover, in window boxes and tubs (when they will behave as trailers, softening hard edges), on walls and fences. There are very many varieties, especially of the common *H. helix*; not all of them are efficient climbers, and a few are propagated from the adult, shrubby state which ivy achieves when it has reached the top of its support. Everyone must have seen an ivy-clad wall, the vertical surface covered with root-clinging, leafy stems and the top crowned with the flowering and fruiting stems of the ivy. Most ivies will grow almost anywhere, including dark shady places. They can be increased by cuttings.

Before tackling *Hedera helix*, let us consider some of the large-leaved species, such as *H. canariensis*. The leaves of this Canary Island and North African native are heart-shaped, and the stems are red. 'Gloire de Marengo' is a popular varie-gated kind with leaves in shades of grey and silvery green edged with cream; it is a little tender, better, in cold climates, as a house plant. Given space it can grow to 6 m (20 ft).

The Persian ivy, *H. colchica*, has even bolder leaves, and is much hardier. It can easily grow to 9 m (30 ft) or more. Popular varieties include 'Dentata', with a few sparse teeth to the margins of the heart-shaped leaves; and its variegated forms 'Dentata Variegata', very striking with creamy primrose margins and a pale greyish zone between the yellow and the deep green centre; and 'Sulphur Heart' ('Paddy's Pride'). This displays the reverse variegation, a bold splash of yellow at the centre of the leaf.

The common ivy, *H. helix*, widespread throughout Europe and Asia, growing among trees both on the forest floor and up into the branches, can reach as much as 30 m (100 ft) where there is a tall enough support. Its varieties range from tiny restrained creepers to the massive Irish ivy. The leaves are just as variable, from little barely-lobed arrowheads to wide frilled confections, in plain green or many different variegations.

Having described some other large-leaved ivies, I shall start with the largest of the common ivies before coming to the tinies. The giant is of course 'Hibernica', the Irish ivy, a whopping plant with very large green leaves. It has tremendous vigour, mostly sideways, making it ideal for large-scale ground-cover. Another vigorous one, though modest by comparison, is 'Parsley Crested' ('Cristata'). It has pale glossy green leaves of basically rounded outline, twisted and crimpled at the margins, and taking on rich red tints in winter. It is suitable for walls, fences, and ground-cover.

'Glacier' is a popular old variegated ivy with silvery grey and ivory leaves on red stems. It makes strong growth, and is ideal among brighter companions. The glossy leaves of 'Harald' ('Chicago Variegated') are yellow and green, aging to cream. Its vigorous growth is ideal for walls and fences, trees, or ground-cover. 'Goldheart' (also, incorrectly, called 'Jubilee') has neat triangular or five-pointed leaves with a golden central flash. With its tidy growth it forms almost geometrical patterns on a wall or fence. It keeps its bright colouring even in light shade.

By contrast, 'Angularis Aurea' needs full sun to retain its colour. It is of medium vigour, with young foliage yellow, and older leaves hazed green on yellow, turning chocolate brown in winter. 'Buttercup' is smaller and more uniformly yellow. It needs full sun but can show leaf-scorch in poor dry soils.

Although it has small leaves, dark green with jagged lobes, 'Green Ripple' makes vigorous growth. It turns coppery purple in winter, especially when grown in full sun.

'Tricolor' has a distinct three-colour variegation of green, cream and pink to blackberry purple, the deepest colours showing in winter. It is suitable for walls and fences. So is the elegant 'Heron'. Its leaves are of bird's foot outline, the central lobe very long, the basal pair pointing backwards, bright green with pale veins.

A newer variegated ivy is 'Caecilia' ('Clotted Cream'), with crinkled, white-variegated leaves. 'Cavendishii' has silvery white variegations on rather small, triangular leaves, often pink-flushed in cold weather.

Several ivies are just as well suited to hanging baskets or window boxes as to walls or fences. 'Manda's Crested' ('Curly Locks') has pale green leaves with very wavy margins, reddish beneath and blotched with red in winter. 'Eva' makes bushy growth, with small green and cream leaves cleanly marked, and forward-pointing lobes. Another, rather slow-growing, is 'Goldchild', with butter-yellow and green variegated leaves.

The very adaptable 'Luzii' has smallish leaves with green marbling on yellow ground, not to everyone's taste. There are few arguments about 'Sagittifolia', which makes dense, quick growth bearing dark green, spear-shaped leaves with backward-pointing basal lobes. 'Sagittifolia Variegata' is its cream and green

One of the boldest of ivies is Hedera colchica; *this is the variety 'Sulphur Heart'. Hardy and evergreen, it grows equally well in sun or shade, and brings colour to the gloomiest of winter days. For a stunning effect in autumn, pair it with Virginia creeper on a high wall.*

Opposite: *There is nothing quite like* Actinidia kolomikta, *a relative of the Kiwi fruit. This is grown only for its cream, green and pink foliage, as bright as flowers. Cats are attracted to this climber not by the pretty leaves, but by some substance in the plant, so that if you do not protect the stems they may chew the plant to death.*

form. 'Kolibri' also has leaves shaped like 'Sagittifolia', but marked with white on three shades of green.

'Adam' is a popular and easy, small-leaved variety with white-variegated leaves tinged with pink in winter. It makes bushy growth, suitable for low walls, hanging baskets, window boxes, or as small-scale ground cover. The most distinctive growth belongs to 'Little Diamond'. The small, white-variegated leaves, diamond-shaped on young stems, are borne on stiffly outward-growing branches when growing upright, or radiating out when growing on the flat or in a hanging basket.

There is something very appealing about green-leaved ivies with a characteristic leaf outline. 'Shamrock' has small, dark green, three-lobed leaves of cupped outline, turning coppery in winter. It makes dense growth suitable for hanging baskets or window boxes. Another is 'Très Coupé', with very small, narrow leaves with long pointed central lobe and small side and basal lobes, and a very bushy habit, slow-growing. 'Deltoidea' has thick, dark green leaves with heart-shaped bases, on stiff growth. It often turns purplish in winter. A very pretty ivy suitable for shady places is 'Ivalace', with dark green, five-lobed leaves with curled margins, coppery in winter.

Deciduous variegated climbers

One of the prettiest of variegated climbers that does not retain its leaves is *Ampelopsis brevipedunculata* 'Elegans' ('Tricolor'). This mouthful of a name belongs to a rather frail climber with leaves heavily splashed and mottled in cream and pink. It needs a warm, sheltered position, and can be grown in a pot, perhaps to be stood outside as patio decoration in summer. It makes a pretty companion for *Rhodochiton atrosanguineum*, and grows to about 2 m (6 ft). Propagate from late summer cuttings. *Humulus japonicus*, the Japanese hop, is a perennial climber that is easily grown as an annual. Unusually, 'Variegatus', its leaves marked with white, comes true from seed.

The bittersweet or woody nightshade, *Solanum dulcamara*, has a form called 'Variegatum'. A scrambling plant of 3 m (10 ft) or so, with pretty foliage heavily variegated with cream, it has small purple potato-flowers in summer followed by red berries, described by Gerard in his famous Herball of 1596 as like 'burnished corall'.

For a climber of more substance, there is *Actinidia kolomikta*. Unlike the Chinese gooseberry, this is grown purely for its foliage. The large, heart-shaped leaves are often, but not always, half green, half cream, flushed with pink. Plants on sunny walls should develop the best colouring, which is also best early in the season. It is only moderately vigorous, reaching about 3 m (10 ft). Cats love it and chew the stems, which should be protected. New plants can be raised from heel cuttings taken in late summer and given bottom heat. The related *A. polygama*, much more uncommon, is called the silver vine because the more tapered leaves are sometimes tipped with white or cream; occasionally a whole leaf is white. It grows to 4.5 m (15 ft).

GREEN AND BEAUTIFUL

Green foliage can be just as beautiful as coloured: perhaps even more so, for we need the repose of green in the garden to contrast with and soothe bright colours. Several handsome climbers for foliage have already found their way into these pages. This section is to remind you of their worth, and to gather together a few loose ends in the shape of climbers that have not yet found a place.

Actinidia arguta has shining green, oblong leaves up to 10 cm (4 in) long, held on long, pink stalks. Small clusters of fragrant white flowers are borne in summer. It needs much more space than the variegated actinidias just described, growing to 10 m (33 ft) or more.

When leaves are described as like those of a vine, the image is of the grape vine's broad, palmate leaves. *Ampelopsis megalophylla* has the largest leaves of any vine. Unusually, they are pinnate, that is with separate leaflets attached to a central stem, or sometimes bipinnate — twice-divided in this way. Deep green above and bluish beneath, they may be as much as 60 cm (2 ft) long. Increase by late summer cuttings.

Aristolochia durior (*A. macrophylla*, *A. sipho*) is the Dutchman's pipe, which has its name from the shape of the curious yellow-green flowers, the lobes edged with purple. The handsome, pale green leaves are kidney-shaped. A quick grower to 6 m (20 ft), it is ideal for walls or pergolas. It is raised from seed, or you can take summer cuttings, which need bottom heat.

9
A VARIETY SHOW OF CLIMBERS

CLIMBERS CAN BE IMMENSELY useful in extending the flowering season in our gardens without occupying much ground space.

Some of the most valuable climbers for getting double value from each patch of soil are the herbaceous and annual or biennial kinds. The latter especially give us a chance to try new combinations without the upheaval of moving a woody-stemmed climber. The fact that the host plant is not encumbered with permanent twining stems may also be an advantage; at the year's end, a cut or two with the knife enables you to pull out dead stems, leaving the host to show its winter tracery.

There are also several climbers that do not fit neatly into the categories I have devised. The fact that they lack fragrance, however, or lose their leaves in winter without flaring in autumn into bonfire colours, or bear no showy fruits, does not mean they are not worth growing.

HERBACEOUS CLIMBERS

These are a varied lot, united only in their herbaceous, non-woody nature. Several can well be used in the border, rather as suggested for sweet peas and their perennial cousins.

The great white bindweed, though undeniably handsome, is a bad weed. But there are two very similar twining bindweeds, *Convolvulus althaeoides* and *C. elegantissimus*, which although rather rampant, are very desirable on account of their silvery foliage and clear pink, satin-finished flowers in summer. If given support they grow to 1 m (3 ft) or more, or they will grow sideways with equal ease.

The double Japanese bindweed, *Calystegia hederacea* 'Flore Pleno', has rosette-shaped pink flowers in summer. It needs rich soil and a sheltered position. In very warm climates, it is true, it may become rather invasive, growing to 4.5 m (15 ft) where suited. Propagate by division.

The climbing 'nasturtiums' attach themselves by twining leaf stalks. Although

Opposite: *The Chilean glory vine,* Eccremocarpus scaber, *is a perennial often grown as an annual; it is now available not only in this typical clear orange, but also in crimson, amber and shades of pink. Here it flowers with the creamy froth of a pyracantha; it will still be in bloom when the firethorn's flowers have turned to bright berries.*

the most familiar is known as the Scottish flame flower, they are all natives of South and Central America. One is as good at sideways as at upwards growth, and can be used as unusual and effective ground cover in the border. *T. tuberosum* is a vigorous plant, with edible tubers which multiply rapidly. The rounded leaves are lobed; the orange and yellow flowers are quite large, though smaller than those of a bedding 'nasturtium' and less widely flared at the mouth. They are borne during summer and autumn, but some forms barely make it before the autumn frosts in cool climates. Choose a variety such as 'Ken Aslet' to be sure of flowers. In cold areas, lift the top layer of tubers in autumn and keep them barely moist and frost-free during the winter. Protect the remaining tubers with a thick covering of grit or ground bark. Plant fresh tubers in spring, in full sun and shelter.

The Scottish flame flower is *T. speciosum*, a slender climber with neat, fresh green leaves on frail stems to 2 m (6 ft), and vivid blood-scarlet flowers in late summer. It is best against a dark background such as a yew hedge, in cool soil, preferably lime-free. The flowers may be followed by indigo-blue berries from which new plants can be raised. The fleshy roots should be planted horizontally about 8 cm (3 in) deep. Propagate by root cuttings, or seed. *T. tricolorum* has even frailer-seeming stems and leaves, and flowers like little scarlet and black tadpoles, in summer. It grows to about 1 m (3 ft), and is increased by division of the tubers.

Another herbaceous climber with edible, tuberous roots is *Apios americana*, introduced to Europe from North America at about the same time as the potato. The pea-flowers are fragrant, sombrely coloured in blood red and mauve-brown, in autumn, on 2 m (6 ft) stems. Increase by division of the tubers.

The climbing alstroemerias or *Bomarea*, like the more familiar border plant itself, are from South America. They need a warm position, in sun. They have twining or scrambling stems to 3 m (10 ft) and tuberous roots, and their flowers are held in clusters. They can be divided, or raised from seed. Perhaps the least uncommon is *B. caldasii*. The flowers are yellow flushed with red, or entirely orange or red; the inner tepals are often spotted with tan or green.

Like woody-stemmed climbers, those that die down in winter can help to extend into autumn the season of interest in the border. *Aconitum volubile* is a climbing monkshood with twining stems, bearing typical hooded flowers of lilac-purple or slaty mauve in late summer and autumn, on 3 m (10 ft) stems. Like the ordinary monkshoods, it prefers a moist soil, in sun or shade. It combines prettily with *Escallonia* 'Edinensis'. Propagate from seed or by division.

Other herbaceous climbers are perhaps better among shrubs, where they will be sheltered from cold winds. It is certainly true of *Codonopsis*, which needs a cool soil in part shade. These enchanting twining plants are related to the campanulas. Many of them have bell-shaped flowers with intriguing markings inside; others are wide-eyed like little clematis flowers. Most are tuberous-rooted, and some have a curious odour, like foxy garlic, when bruised. Most are quite modest in size and can be grown among smallish shrubs. They can be raised from seed.

The codonopsis with wide-open flowers are more immediately striking. *C. convolvulacea* is a twiner, growing to 2 m (6 ft). The flowers are starry, and vary from mid to rich blue. There is also a charming white form, 'Alba'. *C. forrestii* is very similar, but more vigorous to 3.5 m (11 ft), with flowers up to 5 cm (2 in) wide, clear periwinkle blue with darker veins and a bold red-purple eye. Much more delicate in growth is *C. vinciflora*, the twining stems reaching only 1 m (3 ft) or so. The flowers are wide rather like *Vinca*, the periwinkle, but more starry; their colour is very like the blue of a periwinkle, too.

C. tangshen has vigorous twining stems to 3m (10 ft), set with greenish flared bells, the interior spotted and striped with purple. It is irresistible to lovers of green flowers. Most of the remainder are clump-forming, but I cannot omit *C. clematidea*. Not a true climber, it will scramble up to 1 m (3 ft) through neighbouring shrubs. The nodding bells are pale blue, with a ring of orange and maroon-purple inside near the base, the purple faintly showing through to the outside. They open in late summer. The leaves are greyish green.

Another herbaceous climber which needs cool, sheltered conditions is *Dicentra macrocapnos*. Its dangling lockets are shaped like those of the bleeding heart, but are a clear yellow, over a long summer season, amid pale green, divided leaves. The stems will scramble up to 2 m (6 ft) through neighbouring shrubs. In cold areas, protect the roots in winter. Increase from seed. *D. scandens* is similar, climbing by tendrils and bearing flowers for weeks in summer and early autumn.

A climber which is often grown as an annual in cold areas is *Eccremocarpus scaber*. In mild areas the stems are permanent, but elsewhere this Chilean climber will usually grow from the roots even if cut down by frost. It also sows itself freely. The flowers are narrow, lopsidedly bottle-shaped, usually clear orange with yellow lobes, and are borne over a long summer and autumn season. *E. s. aurantiacus* is a form with warm amber yellow flowers; *coccineus* is coppery crimson with dark foliage, and *roseus* has pinkish flowers. All climb by leaf tendrils to 4 m or so.

ANNUAL AND BIENNIAL CLIMBERS

As you may guess from the inclusion of *Eccremocarpus scaber* in the previous section, the borderline between categories of plant is often blurred. Many of those loosely called annuals are in fact perennials from warm climates. They grow quickly enough from seed, however, to be treated as annuals where the winters are too cold for them to survive. This makes them ideal for quick cover while more permanent climbers are making their main growth, as well as for year-by-year changes to your borders. They are also valuable for masking the bare lower limbs of mature climbers. Often they can be grown in pots, trained up a tripod of canes.

Cobaea scandens is just the sort of plant I mean, a climber from Mexico, with tubby bells of greenish-white deepening to violet, borne during summer and autumn. It has a beautiful white form, 'Alba'. The plant climbs by means of tendrils at the ends of the pinnate leaves, to a height of 2–3 m (6–10 ft) when grown as an annual. Pinch out the growing tips regularly to encourage bushy growth.

Another Mexican climber of similar character is *Rhodochiton atrosanguineum*, this one attaching itself by twining leaf stalks and growing to a height of 3 m (10 ft). The flowers are fascinating, composed of a papery, umbrella-shaped calyx of muted red-purple below which hangs a long-tubed, deepest purple-black corolla with five flared lobes. The leaves are heart-shaped, deep green with purple flush.

Bindweed is a word to strike a chill in gardeners' hearts, but Convolvulus elegantissimus, *though vigorous, is no pernicious weed. The silky pink trumpets are set off by finely divided, silvery foliage. Half sprawler, half twining climber, it is ideal at the front of a group of silver and grey-leaved plants with pink, mauve and lilac flowers.*

Puffy balloon-like capsules of seeds follow the flowers. It needs sun and shelter.

Central America is a rich source of good plants for gardens. The asarinas are climbing snapdragons, easy from seed. *Asarina antirrhiniflora* (*Maurandya antirrhiniflora*) has slender stems with neat leaves and red-purple flowers like open-mouthed snapdragons, in summer. It needs sun and shelter, and grows to 1–2 m (3–6 ft). The other species are usually taller, up to 3 m (10 ft), with flowers rather like large foxgloves. Those of *A. barclayana* (*M. barclayana*) are purple, pink or white, and appear over a long season. The heart-shaped leaves are soft-textured. *A. erubescens* (*M. erubescens*) is known as the creeping gloxinia; it has rather sticky, grey-green leaves and large rose-pink flowers in summer and early autumn. *A. scandens* (*M. scandens*), is similar to *A. barclayana*, but with lavender-blue flowers.

As well as sweet peas, the pea family has given us several good garden climbers. *Pueraria lobata*, the kudzu vine, is related to the runner bean, and bears its fragrant, magenta-purple pea flowers in long spikes in summer. Gardeners in cool climates may admire it and grow it as an annual, but in the southern United States it is a bad weed as much as 4.5 m (15 ft) tall. The hyacinth bean, *Lablab purpureus* (*Dolichos lablab*) is a twining climber that also looks rather like the runner bean, with purple or white pea-flowers in long spikes in summer. The young pods and the dried beans can be eaten. It grows to 3 m (10 ft). *Clitoria mariana* bears upside-down, lilac pea-flowers in summer, on twining stems to 1 m (3 ft).

The Canary creeper, *Tropaeolum peregrinum*, is in fact South American. The deeply divided, greyish-green leaves set off bright yellow flowers with fringed tips, in summer. It is beautiful coiling through grey-leaved shrubs, where it can reach 4 m (13 ft). *T. majus*, the common garden 'nasturtium', can itself be a climber or trailer to 2 m (6 ft).

Thunbergia alata, the black-eyed Susan, is a climber from tropical Africa with five-petalled flowers, usually yellow or orange, sometimes cream or ivory-white, with a black-purple 'eye'. A showy and long-lasting annual for sun and shelter, it grows to 3 m (10 ft).

Exceptionally among annuals and biennials, *Adlumia fungosa* needs shade, and shelter from cold winds. It is a climbing fumitory, with little pinky-mauve, spurred flowers and dainty, finely cut foliage. A biennial, it forms in its first winter a rosette of leaves, with second-year flowering stems reaching 1.5 m (5 ft).

Morning glories

The morning glories, species of *Ipomoea*, are tropical plants that climb by twining stems, and need a warm position in sun. A sheltered, sunny wall is ideal. The one

Few can resist the morning glory, Ipomoea tricolor *'Heavenly Blue'. There is nothing quite like the sky blue of its wide funnels, and nothing better than a cloudless blue sky as a setting for the summer-long succession of flowers.*

with clear turquoise flowers is *I. tricolor* 'Heavenly Blue'. Other forms have the same wide funnels, in red-purple, sky or porcelain blue, borne from summer to autumn. They open with the morning sun and fade by mid-afternoon. 'Flying Saucers' is striped in blue and white. They grow to 3–4.5 m (10–15 ft).

I. learii (*I. acuminata*, *Pharbitis learii*), the blue dawn flower, has blue or violet flowers in clusters, and heart-shaped or lobed leaves. It grows vigorously to 12 m (40 ft) in the tropics, less in cooler climates. Sun and shelter also suit *I. nil* (*Ph. nil*), which bears purple, violet, blue, lavender, maroon or red flowers in summer. Several strains, single or double-flowered, have been developed.

The common morning glory, *I. purpurea*, is a hardier plant than the last two, and bears many purple flowers in summer. White, pink, magenta and violet forms are also known. The leaves are heart-shaped, on stems to 3–4.5 m (10–15 ft).

The moonflower has been renamed *Calonyction aculeatum* (formerly *Ipomoea bona-nox*). Its white, perfumed flowers up to 15 cm (6 in) wide open in the evening. It is a plant for a warm, sheltered position, or conservatory.

Not all ipomoeas have blue or purple or white flowers. *I. coccinea* (*Quamoclit coccinea*), the star glory, bears its bright scarlet, fragrant flowers in clusters during summer and early autumn. Then there is *I. quamoclit* (*Quamoclit pennata*), the cypress vine, which has foliage finely cut into feathery segments. The flowers are scarlet and open from summer to autumn. Like the last, it grows to 3 m. *Mina lobata* is related to the morning glories. This Mexican climber has curving, tubular flowers that open crimson-scarlet, fading through orange to primrose and ivory. They are borne on one-sided sprays during summer and early autumn. The leaves are three-lobed, and the twining stems reach 3–4 m (10–13 ft).

A MIXED BAG OF WOODY CLIMBERS

The quality that unites the climbers which follow is simply that they have refused to fit into my categories. The rest of the climbing hydrangeas, for example, must not slip through the net just because they are not evergreen. *Hydrangea petiolaris* is a deciduous, root-clinging climber, much more showy in flower than its evergreen relative (*H. serratifolia*) (described in Chapter 8), for the white flower-heads bear many sterile florets to give the familiar lacecap effect, in summer. It is hardy and suitable for shady walls, tree trunks, large stumps, or spreading ground-cover. As a climber it reaches 10 m (33 ft) or more. Layers form roots readily, or you can take cuttings in late summer.

The schizophragmas, like *H. petiolaris*, have self-clinging stems and are happy in shady places, though they flower more freely in sun. They are deciduous. The flower-heads are 'lacecaps', but the small fertile florets are surrounded by large, showy bracts so the effect is bolder. Propagation is as for *H. petiolaris*. In *Schizo-phragma hydrangeoides* the wide flower-heads have cream bracts, or pink in the variety 'Roseum', and appear in summer. It is a fine wall plant, which can also be grown up the trunk of a tree as in the wild. Choose a tree with a tall trunk free of low branches, for the climber may reach 12 m (40 ft). The flower-heads of *S. integri-folium* are larger, and the ivory-cream bracts are bolder and long-lasting. In its native China it grows in cool, damp valleys, clinging to rocky cliffs.

The Russian vine or mile-a-minute vine, *Polygonum baldschuanicum* (*Fallopia baldschuanica*), is an extremely vigorous, twining climber to 12 m (40 ft) with heart-shaped leaves. It can be quite showy in summer when bearing its sprays of many tiny, white or pink-tinged flowers, but is a plant for roughish places, in sun or half-shade. If you should actually want more than one, take cuttings.

Surprisingly, the Russian vine is related to *Muehlenbeckia axillaris*, a creeping or scrambling plant from New Zealand, with slender, intertwining, dark stems set with small, sparse leaves. It is best used as ground-cover, spreading to 1 m (3 ft) or so. *M. complexa* is more of a climber, very vigorous especially in milder areas, making a wide-spreading tangle of black stems if grown without support, or reaching up to 6 m (20 ft). The leaves may be rounded or heart-shaped, or in the variety *trilobata* they are fiddle-shaped. This is certainly not a showy species, but is curiously attractive in a wildish corner. Sun or shade suit it. Both muehlenbeckias are propagated from summer cuttings.

For something more spectacular, turn to *Solanum crispum*. The climbing potatoes are mostly rather tender, but this species is hardy except in the coldest areas. The potato-like flowers are bright violet, enlivened by a cone of yellow stamens at the centre. The best variety to choose is 'Glasnevin', which has a very long summer and autumn season. It can be trained against a wall, or allowed to ramble through supporting shrubs, reaching 4.5 m (15 ft). Take late summer cuttings.

For late colour, there is *Senecio scandens*. This climbing daisy is valuable because it flowers in autumn, until the frosts. The scrambling stems are set with pale bright green foliage. The flowers are little lemon yellow daisies, borne with great freedom in clusters. A dark background is the ideal complement. Some shelter is needed, though if the stems are cut by frost the plant will shoot again from the base. It will grow up to 4.5 m if not cut by frost, and is easy from cuttings.

CLIMBERS FOR FRUIT

Climbers with edible fruits may be attractive enough to grow as ornamentals as well: the Chinese gooseberry, for example, is handsome in leaf. When you grow a climber for its ornamental fruits, however, you will need to think of display, not flavour. Whereas autumn foliage is best seen with the sun behind it, you need to arrange things in exactly the opposite way for fruits. Seen against the light, they are just dark blobs. But where the sun strikes them, they come to life.

Edible

Let us start with edible fruits. *Actinidia deliciosa* (*A. chinensis*), the Chinese goose-berry, is now known as the Kiwi fruit, which is a shame as its origin is Chinese. A vigorous climber to 9 m (30 ft), it is cultivated for its now familar furry brown fruits with a sweet, fresh, green pulp. You need male and female plants for a crop of fruit, and will get bigger and better 'gooseberries' from a named variety such as 'Hayward'. The flowers are fragrant, white clusters turning to buff. The heart-shaped leaves, larger on non-fruiting branches, are handsome. To keep varieties true to name, take cuttings in late summer and give them bottom heat.

The vines, above all, are *the* fruiting climbers. *Vitis* 'Brant' is derived from the grape vine, with sweet black grapes and coppery purple autumn colour with the veins picked out in green. It grows to 6 m (20 ft). For the propagation of this and the grape vine varieties, turn to Chapter 4 where eye cuttings are described.

The original grape vine is *V. vinifera*, so long cultivated that its origins are lost in time, but known throughout the Mediterranean world. There are many kinds developed for their fruiting and vineyard qualities, including some that could be tried in cool-temperate climates:

> 'Black Hamburgh' (black — glasshouse in cool areas)
> 'Chasselas' (white — glasshouse or outdoor)
> 'Fragola' (red, strawberry-flavoured — outdoor)
> 'Madelaine Silvaner' (white — outdoor)
> 'Müller-Thurgau' (Riesling-Silvaner, white — outdoor)
> 'Muscat of Alexandria' (white — glasshouse)
> 'Seyval Blanc' (Seyve Villard 5,276, white — outdoor)
> 'Siegerrebe' (white — outdoor)

Ornamental

Ampelopsis is first in the alphabet of vines. One species can be attractive in fruit. *A. brevipenduculata* has hop-like leaves, deep green above and paler beneath. It is best given full sun and a restricted root-run, when it should produce a good crop of small porcelain blue 'grapes', on vigorous growth to 6 m (20 ft) or more. Increase by late summer cuttings.

Another close relation of an edible plant is *Cucurbita pepo ovifera*. This is the ornamental gourd, which produces brightly coloured fruits of varying shapes. They are most often rounded or flagon-shaped, and may be smooth or warty, plain or striped. The skin is hard, so they can be dried for decoration: some people varnish them, to make them shiny and to keep them from shrivelling. New plants are raised afresh each year from seed.

Celastrus orbiculatus, the climbing bettersweet, has great vigour and easily makes a tangle of twining stems, so that it is better grown in informal surroundings, into trees or among large shrubs. The foliage turns yellow in autumn. The fruits resemble small spindleberries, splitting open to reveal scarlet seeds against a shiny yellow background. They last well when picked. To be sure of fruits, though, you need either a male and a female plant, or the hermaphrodite form. Propagate by layers or rooted suckers to be sure of the sex of your plant.

The schisandras are twining climbers from Asia, the females bearing showy scarlet fruits. Schisandras grow best in a partly shaded position in moist, leafy soil. Propagate from late summer cuttings. The showiest of them, and the least uncommon, is *Schisandra rubriflora*. It bears crimson, fragrant flowers in early summer, and scarlet berries in drooping spikes up to 15 cm (6 in), on stems up to 6 m (20 ft). *S. chinensis* is a deciduous climber with fragrant pale pink flowers in spring; the petals drop very quickly. The scarlet fruits are borne in hanging spikes up to 8 cm (3 in) long, and last well into winter. It grows to 9 m (30 ft). You may also like to try *S. sphenanthera*, which has flowers of terracotta and green in late spring, followed by scarlet fruits on short hanging spikes. It reaches 4.5 m (15 ft).

10
WARM WALLS AND CONSERVATORIES

GARDENERS OFTEN TAKE UP THE challenge of growing a plant that is rather tender. A sheltered wall may make it possible to succeed with tender or half-hardy climbers, for the temperature against a wall is higher than in the open garden where the wind can chill. Some cold-sensitive climbers need sun, others shade, so provided other conditions are right, any wall can make a home for one or other of these plants.

Other climbers may be perfectly winter-hardy, but reluctant to flower unless they get plenty of summer sun. Many members of the Bignonia family flower spectacularly well in France or Switzerland or Italy, even where the winters are cold, because the summers are hot and long, but do less well where the winters are milder but the summers usually dull. A wall facing right into the sun is the place to grow them in such a climate.

Climbers that are decidedly tender (a relative term, of course) can be grown in the shelter of a conservatory or glasshouse. Even a conservatory which is kept only just frost free in winter can provide enough protection for many beautiful climbers. With a little more winter heat the range increases, but it seems rather irresponsible to suggest such extravagance unless a way can be found to exploit renewable, non-polluting energy resources. If you do heat, even to the minimum of 5°C (41°F) required to keep out frost, remember that you can save a good deal of energy by efficient insulation: double-glazing, an inner lining of polythene or of bubble plastic. The drawback is that all these will reduce light levels, while if your conservatory becomes virtually airtight as a result of your conservation measures, you will be encouraging a muggy atmosphere where horrid moulds will thrive. Ventilation is also a must.

Sometimes it is hard to decide whether to suggest a particular climber for the conservatory or for a sheltered place outside. So much depends upon the area in which you live, and on the microclimate in your garden. In frost-free climates everything in this chapter will grow outdoors.

CLIMBERS FOR SHELTERED, SUNNY WALLS

As we have seen, a sheltered wall need not necessarily face straight into the sun. One that catches the afternoon sun only may be almost as good, so long as the shelter is there. Several of the climbers that need such shelter in cold climates have already been described: some clematis and jasmines, *Dregea sinensis*, *Mandevilla laxa* and the Banksian roses among them. In warmer climates, many of the climbers in this chapter could well be grown in similar conditions to their hardier relatives already described, rather than needing special protection.

Araujia sericofera is a South American twining climber related to *Dregea*, and known as the cruel plant, because night-flying moths, attracted to the flowers, can be trapped by their tongues in the flowers as they search for nectar. The flowers are fragrant, and may be either white or mauve-pink; they open in summer amid greyish evergreen foliage. *Araujia* is easily raised from seed to flowering size; at maturity it can reach 6 m (20 ft).

As well as *Solanum crispum* already described, the potato family also offers *S. jasminoides*, a climber with slender, twining stems to 6 m (20 ft) set with leaves that smell nasty when bruised. The flowers, though unscented, are extremely pretty, especially in the white form 'Album'. The pure white of the petals is enlivened by the central yellow cone of stamens so typical of the potato family. The white form is more often seen in gardens than the slate-blue colouring which is apparently typical in the wild. The season lasts from summer well into autumn. Increase by late summer cuttings.

A climber related to the holboellias, but more tender, *Lardizabala biternata* is an evergreen twiner growing to 3–4 m (10–13 ft). The chocolate-purple and white flowers open in winter, male blossoms in long hanging spikes and female flowers single. Like its cousins it may produce fleshy purple 'sausages' after a hot summer. Sow seeds, put down layers, or take cuttings, to increase.

Kadsura japonica, an evergreen twining climber from warmer areas of Japan, China and Taiwan, is related to the schisandras. It has narrow leaves tapering to a point, of rich shining green. The fragrant cream flowers in summer are followed by scarlet fruits. It prefers lime-free soil, and grows to 3 m (10 ft). 'Variegata' has cream-margined leaves. Propagate by late summer cuttings.

The daisy family is very varied, ranging from annuals (including some bad weeds) to tall shrubs. The climbing daisies or *Mutisia* of South America are worth cherishing for their brilliant colours, though they are not the easiest climbers to please. They attach themselves by leaf tendrils. Many spread by suckering stems once established. Never be tempted to dig up suckers as a way to increase the plant. The likelihood is that both the detached sucker and the mother plant will die. If you want to make new plants, sow seed or take cuttings in summer. Give your mutisia rich soil and sun, and a shrub to support its stems and shade its roots.

One of the easier species is *M. ilicifolia*, with toothed, holly-like leaves, and mauve-pink daisies from spring to late summer. Dead leaves tend to clutter the plant. Against a wall it should be safe from what it most dislikes, cold wet soils in winter. It grows to around 3 m (10 ft), whereas *M. oligodon* is more of a suckering trailer of 1.5 m (5 ft) than a true climber, with spine toothed leaves and clear pink, satin-finished daisies from summer to autumn. *M. retusa* is a taller climber, up to 6 m (20 ft), with pink daisies among leaves that vary from somewhat to not at all toothed. As well as the species described, look out for *M. decurrens* and *M. clematis*, both of which have brilliant orange daisies and are rather tricky to establish.

Two slender climbers from the antipodes are ideal where space is limited. *Billardiera longifolia* is a slender twining climber growing to 2 m (6 ft), with pretty lime-green bell-flowers in summer. The fruits are its true attraction, however. They are oblong berries of deep royal blue (or sometimes white or red). Although they look fleshy, when you shake them the seeds rattle inside what is actually a dry capsule. Sow these seeds to make new plants. Neutral to acid soil in sun or part shade suits the billiardieras.

The sollyas are Australian climbers of very slender, twining growth, needing a warm sheltered wall. *S. heterophylla* is the bluebell creeper, with sky blue bells in summer and autumn on 2 m (6 ft) stems. *S. parviflora* is smaller, with richer blue bells and very narrow leaves. Propagate from seed or cuttings.

The passion flowers

Passiflora caerulea, the blue passion flower, was so named by Spanish priests who, finding it growing wild in South America, fancied that the parts of the flower symbolized the instruments of Christ's passion. The ten tepals represent ten apostles, the corona (the ring of filaments within the tepals) the crown of thorns, the five stamens the five wounds and the three stigmas the three nails. It is a very vigorous climber attaching itself by coiling tendrils. In mild winters it will retain its deep green, divided leaves; but even if cut right to the ground by frost, so long as the roots do not freeze it will grow again from the roots in spring. The white or palest blush tepals surround the corona which is brightly zoned in purple, white and blue. The flowering season is long, and after hot summers orange, egg-shaped fruits may form. There is a beautiful white form, 'Constance Elliot'. The blue passion flower grows to 9 m (30 ft) — even in one season if cut back, it can reach 4.5 m (15 ft). Both the blue and white forms can be propagated from summer cuttings.

A hybrid with the beautiful *P. racemosa*, described later in this chapter, *P.* × *caerulea-racemosa*, is almost as hardy as the blue passion flower. It is a rather variable cross, the flowers flushed mauve-pink, with purple corona. It is of equal vigour and flowers over a long summer to autumn season. Another that seems as hardy is *P. umbilicata*, which has amethyst or purple flowers, not large but richly coloured, in summer, and grows to 6 m (20 ft) or more.

CLIMBERS FOR WARM SHADE

For the climbers that like both shelter and shade, you need to emulate their native conditions of high atmospheric humidity and the shelter of tall, possibly evergreen trees. Wind is the greatest enemy of these plants, apart from severe frost. They may also be damaged by too much sun, for their leaves are often thin-textured and ill-equipped to resist scorch. As you would expect, they prefer, or even insist on, a leafy soil, which will usually be neutral to acid.

The Gesneria family, the same which includes the familiar house plant known as gloxinia, offers two or three almost hardy climbers that need just such leafy, shady conditions. The easiest is *Mitraria coccinea*, more of a scrambler than a climber. The flowers, which open in summer and autumn, are bright, lopsided trumpets of furry texture and vivid orange-scarlet colouring. The leaves are small, neat and evergreen. Mitraria does very well scrambling through shrubs in a sheltered, shady place, or it can be tied in to a wall or tree trunk. Summer cuttings root easily.

For something more challenging, try *Asteranthera ovata*. This is a self-clinging evergreen from Chile, where it grows up tree trunks in quite dense forest. At first, if you can persuade it to settle in moist, leafy soil in a shady corner, it will grow sideways, when each pair of thin, bristly leaves grows at right angles to the next. As it begins to climb, they flatten into one plane so that the stem roots can do their work. The flowers are tubular, with five flared lobes, their colour deep crushed-strawberry pink with deeper veinings and a white throat, opening from mid summer. In the wild it reaches quite high up its tall host trees, but in captivity I have not seen it over 4 m (13 ft) at most. Grow from cuttings.

Another Chilean climber, this one related to the lilies, is *Lapageria rosea*, an evergreen with twining stems and leaves shaped like long slender hearts. The flowers are exquisite, high-shouldered waxy bells of long, slightly flared outline. They are usually soft crimson-pink, but there is a white form, *L. albiflora*. 'White Cloud' is an especially good selection from this. 'Nash Court' has larger bells of paler pink flecked with rose, and 'Flesh Pink' is another pale form. They all need shelter, especially from cold winds, and a leafy soil. New plants can be raised from fresh seed, but to remain true to type, named kinds must be layered.

Ficus pumila, the climbing fig, is almost hardy, and will stand a degree or two of frost. It will grow well even in dense shade, climbing like ivy by stem roots up to 4 m (13 ft). Like ivy it has a juvenile, climbing stage and an adult, shrubby stage. The juvenile stems are slender and bear small heart-shaped leaves, closely set. Increase by summer cuttings.

CLIMBERS FOR CONSERVATORIES AND FROST-FREE GARDENS

The climbers grouped here vary in their need for heat in winter. I will try to indicate the winter minimum temperature for each. There are also some climbers which have already been described, for they are reasonably hardy, yet which may be worth growing under cover in cold gardens, for example, *Clematis cirrhosa*, which flowers in winter. Under glass, not only are its discreet freckled bells protected from the elements, but you will be able to enjoy its lemon fragrance. Several jasmines make beautiful plants for the conservatory, where their perfume is held in the still, warm air. Climbers grown as annuals, such as *Cobaea scandens*, can be kept as perennials, making excellent summer shading for the conservatory and coming into flower much earlier in the season than when raised afresh each year from seed.

Periwinkle family

The periwinkle family has some good things for the conservatory, such as the mandevillas. *Mandevilla × amabilis* 'Alice du Pont' is a hybrid with warm pink

Pure blue is a rare colour in the garden, which may account for the affection many feel for Tweedia caerulea, *a small perennial climber for frost-free conditions. Look closely to see the delicacy of its colouring, pale turquoise flowers aging towards lilac and mauve, among velvety grey foliage.*

flowers, much larger than those of *M. laxa* (see Chapter 7). It has a delicate fragrance, and needs a winter minimum of 7–10°C (45–50°F). Take cuttings in summer: as this is a hybrid it will not come true from seed. The same winter minimum should see *M. sanderi* safely through. The rose-pink flowers with a yellow eye open chiefly in summer, but as they depend on temperature (minimum 15°C [59°F]) rather than day length they may appear at almost any time. It can grow up to 4.5 m (15 ft). *M. splendens* (*Dipladenia splendens*) is a twining climber of slighter growth than this, with larger flowers, often more than 10 cm (4 in) wide, of pink to carmine, in summer. The roots are tuberous so the plant can be kept nearly dry in winter while dormant, but should be given a minimum temperature of 7–10°C (45–50°F). It makes a fine pot plant, and can grow to 3 m (10 ft).

From Central America comes another climber in the periwinkle family, *Allamanda cathartica*. The flowers, borne in clusters in summer and autumn, are rich yellow trumpets with spreading lobes. It is a scrambler rather than a true climber, with stems up to 9 m (30 ft) and evergreen leaves. It is at its best when trained upwards, the flowering sprays allowed to hang down from a height. Grow in a tub if you need to restrict its growth, and give it a minimum winter temperature of 13°C (55°F). Spring or summer cuttings root well with bottom heat.

Beaumontia grandiflora is yet another twining, climbing member of the periwinkle family, this time from India. The flowers are long, sweet-scented, white trumpets, borne in clusters in early summer. Grow it in a peaty soil, kept dryish in winter, with a minimum temperature of 7–10°C (45–50°F). The young shoots are rust-coloured and furry, the leaves are large and glossy. It can grow up to 12 m (40 ft) in warm humid climates, and is raised from summer cuttings.

More tender passion flowers

In frost-free conditions, there are several beautiful passion flowers to choose from. All can be increased by summer cuttings, or you could try growing them from seed, but hybrids will not come true. They are all tendril climbers.

One group, which used to be known as the tacsonias, has long-tubed flowers. *Passiflora antioquiensis* is one of the most opulent of this group, bearing spectacular rich red flowers with violet corona, in late summer and autumn. Keep just frost-free in winter. It grows to 6 m (20 ft) or more. *P. mollissima* is quite a weed in warm countries, but beautiful with its long-tubed pink flowers and downy leaves on 7.5 m (25 ft) stems. Give it a winter minimum of 5°C (41°F). The cross between the two is *P. × exoniensis*, which has showy rose-pink flowers very freely borne. It grows vigorously to 9 m (30 ft), and needs a winter minimum of 5°C (41°F).

Passion flowers can produce passion fruit. *P. edulis*, the granadilla, is the common passion fruit that can be bought in greengrocers' shops. The large white flowers have a corona of curly white, violet-banded filaments, and open in summer. It has three-lobed leaves on vigorous stems up to 6 m (20 ft) or more. Give it a winter minimum of 5°C (41°F). The giant granadilla is *P. quadrangularis*, a vigorous climber to 6 m (20 ft) with very large, cupped flowers, white, pink or mauve with a corona formed of very long filaments, wavy and banded with purple. In hot countries the big yellow fruits, that look rather like melons, are used to make a refreshing drink. It needs a winter minimum of 7–10°C (45–50°F).

Passiflora 'Allardii' is a cross between the white 'Constance Elliott' and *P. quadrangularis*, with large white, pink-flushed flowers, the corona banded with white and blue. It is nearly as hardy as the first parent; it reaches 4.5 m (15 ft).

A passion flower with a difference is *P. racemosa*. Unlike the others, it bears its starry, scarlet flowers in racemes, not singly. They have purple filaments. It is a showy and beautiful climber, quite rampant when grown outside in warm climates, but reasonably restrained under glass, perhaps 4 m (13 ft). Provide a winter minimum of 5°C (41°F).

Tetrapathaea tetrandra is in effect a passion flower, but its native land is New Zealand, not South America. The small, greenish-yellow flowers cannot stand comparison with the true passion flowers, but on female plants the bright orange, pear-shaped fruits, 3 cm (1 in) long, are very showy. You need, of course, a male plant as well to obtain fruits. The foliage is evergreen and the stems reach 9 m (30 ft). Sow seeds in spring or take cuttings in summer, give it a humus-rich, neutral or acid soil, and keep it just frost-free in winter.

Pea family

From warm climates come several showy climbing members of the pea family, ideal for conservatories in cold areas. *Clitoria terneata* has clear bright blue flowers on twining stems. It is evergreen, and needs a winter minimum of 7–10°C (45–50°F). The hardenbergias, from Australia, are hardier, needing a minimum winter temperature of only 5°C (41°F). They can be increased by seed or by summer cuttings. They are sometimes called native wisteria. *Hardenbergia comptoniana* has sprays of small violet-blue flowers in spring; the variety *rosea* is pink. The deeper violet *H. violacea* is also known in pink or white. The flowers always bear a yellow blotch. Both grow to 3 m (10 ft).

Another collection of Australian climbing pea flowers, needing similar conditions to the hardenbergias and all easily raised from seed, are the kennedias. *Kennedia coccinea* is the coral pea, with vivid scarlet flowers in spring. It reaches 2 m (6 ft) as a climber, or it will grow as a trailer. Another red-flowered climber-cum-sprawler is *K. eximia*. In *K. rubicunda* the drooping sprays are composed of dusky red pea-flowers, opening in early summer. The young foliage is covered in tawny down. It grows to around 3 m (10 ft), as does *K. nigricans*. This, the black coral pea, is not showy, but its chocolate-maroon and yellow flowers are fascinating.

Trumpet vines

The bignonias or trumpet vines have been separated by the botanists into several different genera, but many gardeners still use the familiar name bignonia. The winter-hardy ones will come later in the chapter; here I want to concentrate on those that need a frost-free climate or conservatory protection.

One of the most spectacular is *Pyrostegia venusta*, known as golden shower on account of its rich orange-yellow funnels, borne in clusters in late winter and spring. It is a tendril climber, at its best in mild climates where it can scale a tree or high wall, growing up to 9 m (30 ft), and cascade down. It will also sprawl on the ground and flower just as freely. Propagate by summer cuttings, and give it a winter minimum of 5–10°C (41–50°F).

The Cape honeysuckle, *Tecomaria capensis*, is another bignonia despite its common name, with twining stems, forming bushy growth. The flowers are brilliant orange-scarlet trumpets borne in terminal spikes from spring to autumn. The dark, glossy leaves are composed of several leaflets. Increase by summer cuttings. Rich moist soil and a humid atmosphere encourage it to climb to 4.5 m (15 ft) or more. It needs a winter minimum of 5°C (41°F).

Barely a climber, the bower vine from Australia, *Pandorea jasminoides*, may slowly make twining growth to 2 m (6 ft), or remain loosely shrubby. The wide-mouthed trumpet flowers are pink or white, with a showy crimson eye — 'Rosea Superba' is a well-coloured form. They open in summer and autumn among dark green, polished foliage. Increase by summer cuttings, and give it the same winter protection as the Cape honeysuckle. *P. pandorana* extends from Australia to New Guinea, and is known as the wonga-wonga vine, from its aboriginal name. It is much more vigorous than the bower vine, up to 6 m (20 ft), with smaller but very abundant, fragrant flowers, cream with a blotch of crimson in the throat, over a

Upper: *The glory lily,* Gloriosa superba, *despite its exotic appearance, is not difficult so long as it can be kept frost-free in winter. It hoists itself up by little hooks at the tips of the leaves.*

Lower: *In high latitude gardens the trumpet vines need plenty of sun to flower well, so they must have a wall facing straight into the midday sun. But in areas with hotter summers,* Campsis radicans *and its kin will flower abundantly year after year without any special encouragement, the envy of travellers from colder climes.*

long spring and summer season. Increase by summer cuttings. It needs a slightly higher winter minimum of 7°C (45°F).

Podrania ricasoliana is a southern African climber similar to *Pandorea*, with pinnate leaves and fragrant trumpets of rose-pink veined with crimson, in summer. Evergreen in frost-free conditions, it will stand a degree or two of frost, when it becomes deciduous. It grows to 3 m (10 ft).

Tender herbaceous and sub-shrubby climbers

One of the most appealing climbers for warm conditions is *Tweedia caerulea* (*Oxypetalum caeruleum*). A delightful twining perennial climber from South America, it has thick-textured sky-blue, star-shaped flowers and greyish, downy foliage, making its own gentle colour scheme. The flowers age towards pinkish-lilac. It can be propagated by spring cuttings of basal growths, and may also be grown annually from seed, reaching 1 m (3 ft). It requires a winter minimum of 5°C (41°F).

Small-sized climbers such as this are especially valuable where conservatory space in limited. The glory lily, *Gloriosa superba*, like tweedia, can be grown in a pot and takes little room. It has tuberous roots, characteristically V-shaped, which can be stored dry at 7°C (45°F) in winter. In spring they should be started into growth, and can be kept under cover or stood out during summer, provided with supports for its 2 m (6 ft) growths. The slender stems are set with narrow leaves bearing little hooks at their tips. Each flower is like a wavy-petalled Turk's cap lily, opening yellow and deepening to red with age. Increase by offset tubers.

Sandersonia aurantiaca is a climber related to and resembling the gloriosas, but growing to only 60 cm (2 ft). It has curious flowers like little tubby lanterns, pale tangerine-orange in colour. An ideal pot plant, it has the same needs as the gloriosas. So too does *Littonia modesta*, a charming little climber like a small *Gloriosa*, with nodding, clear orange, bowl-shaped flowers in summer.

The usual image of a campanula is a blue-flowered border or rock plant. But *Canarina canariensis* is a climbing campanula, with tuberous roots and waxy orange bells from late autumn to spring. It is summer-dormant and can be dried off to start into growth again in autumn, to be kept at a winter minimum of 10°C (50°F). The leaves are narrow, toothed triangles of fresh green on growth to 2 m (6 ft). It is easy from seed.

Sometimes it is fun to grow a plant that is bizarre rather than beautiful. This description could apply to the ceropegias, tropical and subtropical perennials, of which some are twining climbers and some tuberous-rooted. They have tubular flowers with spreading mouth and petal lobes joined at their tips, making a sort of cage or parachute. Give them a very open, gritty compost, kept almost dry in winter, with a minimum temperature of 10°C (50°F), and grow them in full sun. Look out for names such as *Ceropegia radicans*, *C. stapeliiformis* and *C. sandersonii*, the fountain flower.

A climber with more immediate appeal is *Manettia inflata* (*M. bicolor*). The firecracker vine from South America is a perennial with twining stems to 1 m (3 ft), and lustrous evergreen foliage. The tubular scarlet and yellow flowers are plush-textured, and open over a long spring to autumn season. Propagate by summer cuttings, and ensure a winter minimum of 5°C (41°F).

Climbers common and uncommon

Bougainvillea is one of the most familiar climbers in warm areas, from the Mediterranean to the Indian subcontinent, from California to Florida, in short wherever the winters are virtually or wholly frost-free. It is a scrambler rather than a true climber. The showy part of the bloom is not the actual flowers, but the bright bracts surrounding them. These may be the typical assertive magenta, or range from white and ivory and soft yellow through shades of pink, coral and orange to pure scarlet and crimson, purple and mauve. There are literally dozens of named varieties, including at least one with variegated leaves. All can be quite easily increased by summer cuttings. Grown in pots they can be kept quite small; allowed to roam freely, they can reach 6 m (20 ft) or more. A sunny position encourages flowering. They need a winter minimum of 7–10°C (45–50°F), though they will survive short periods at lower temperatures.

Something much more unusual is *Anredera cordifolia*, a tuberous-rooted, twining climber from South America, which used to rejoice in the name of *Boussingaultia baselloides*. The little white flowers, fragrant like mignonette, open in autumn and have given it an easier name, the mignonette vine. Small aerial tubers form in the non-flowering leaf axils and can be grown on to make new plants. To survive it needs a winter minimum of 5°C (41°F); in warmer temperatures, whether artificial or natural, it does not stop growing all year, to reach 6 m (20 ft).

Another scented climber needing warmth is *Gelsemium sempervirens*. The false jasmine or evening trumpet flower is a beautiful climber from the south-eastern United States, where because the summers are long and hot it can stand a mild winter frost. In cool climates, where the summers are duller, it makes softer growth and must be kept frost-free in winter. The narrow, polished evergreen leaves are borne on twining stems growing to 3–6 m (10–20 ft). In summer, fragrant flowers of jasmine-like shape, varying from deep to pale yellow, are borne in clusters. There is a double-flowered form. Increase by summer cuttings.

Another group of evergreen climbers, the hibbertias from Australia, are able to stand a degree or two of frost (and to grow again from the roots if cut back by cold in winter) but do better in a just frost-free glasshouse in cool climates. They all have yellow flowers of simple, saucer-shaped outline rather like a single rose. Increase by seed or summer cuttings. *Hibbertia dentata* has clear yellow flowers opening in summer. The coppery-green leaves are toothed, and borne on pinkish stems growing to 3 m (10 ft). In the wild it grows in moist eucalyptus forests. *H. scandens* (*H. volubilis*) is a more determined climber, with bronzed foliage, brighter yellow flowers all summer, and twining stems to 4.5 m (13 ft).

If your climate is not suitable for growing *Lonicera hildebrandiana* outside, you will need a very large conservatory. This huge honeysuckle, outsized in growth, in leaf and in flower (each flower up to 15 cm [6 in] long) comes from a mild climate, and needs a very warm sheltered site where the winter temperature does not fall below 5°C (41°F). It will grow to 24 m (80 ft) or so. The flowers, borne in summer, are very fragrant; at first white, they age to tawny buff.

Petraea volubilis, though not on the scale of the giant honeysuckle, is another tall climber for milder climates, where it grows up to 9 m (30 ft) tall, with twining stems. It comes from tropical America and is known as purple wreath. The violet flowers in starry, paler lilac calyces are borne in long sprays at almost any season when the temperature is high enough. I have seen it look spectacular in Florida, in May. It needs a rich soil, in sun, can be increased by summer cuttings, and does best with a winter minimum of 7–10°C (45–50°F).

Even *Aristolochia elegans*, a Brazilian relative of the Dutchman's pipe, can grow up to 6 m (20 ft). It is more tender and much more showy than *A. sipho*, with a long succession of wide-mouthed maroon flowers blotched with white, which is presumably why it is called the calico flower. Propagate from summer cuttings with bottom heat, or seed.

A plant that is very familiar to gardeners in cool climates as a bedding or greenhouse plant is *Plumbago auriculata* (*P. capensis*). The blue plumbago is grown for its sky-blue flowers in sprays during a long summer and autumn season. It also comes in white. It is more of a scrambler than a climber, but will reach 4 m (13 ft) high and wide if tied to a support. Increase by summer cuttings. Prune it hard in spring, and keep it just frost-free in winter.

The potato family has its share of good things for the conservatory. The golden chalice vine, *Solandra maxima*, is a Mexican climber with large, fragrant, trumpet-shaped flowers that first open in the evening. At this stage they are pale yellow with five dark purple stripes within. As they age the petal lobes reflex and the colour deepens, until on the third day they are suffused with tawny brown. Sun and rich soil suit this rampant evergreen climber which may reach 50 m (150 ft) in the wild. Propagate by summer cuttings, and allow a winter minimum of 7–10°C (45–50°F).

Streptosolen jamesonii is the marmalade bush, a scrambling climber that can be grown as a pot plant. The flowers are bright orange, flared trumpets, borne in clusters in late spring and summer, amid rich green leaves. Propagate by late summer cuttings. It grows to 2–3 m (6–10 ft) in a tub or greenhouse border. More like the conventional image of a climbing potato is *Solanum wendlandii*, which bears branching clusters of large, blue-lilac flowers in late summer. Increase by summer cuttings, and keep at a winter minimum of 7–10°C (45–50°F), like the marmalade bush.

Climbers as house plants

One of the most popular of house plants in cold climates must be the wax flower, *Hoya carnosa*, on account of its rounded clusters of palest blush, waxy flowers with a crimson eye, which are delectably fragrant, especially at night. They are borne in successive crops over two years or more. The twining stems bear thick, leathery, glossy green foliage, and may reach 4 m (13 ft) if not restricted. Increase by summer cuttings. The winter minimum should be 5°C (41°F), or even a degree or two lower if the plant is kept rather dry.

Climbing house plants are often grown more for their foliage than their flowers. This is certainly true of *Senecio macroglossus*, a climbing ragwort, known as Cape ivy or wax vine. If you combine the names you have a good image of the plant, which has thick, dark green, lustrous leaves. There is a variegated form with yellow-marked leaves, likely to be less vigorous than the green form, which reaches 3 m (10 ft). The flowers are of little account. The Cape ivy needs a winter minimum of 7–10°C (45–50°F), and can be increased by cuttings in summer.

The kangaroo vine, *Cissus antarctica*, a true vine, is a popular house plant in cool regions. It has toothed, shining green leaves and makes a dense leafy mass. It is able to reach 4.5 m (15 ft) or more, but is more restrained when constricted in a pot. It can be propagated by summer cuttings, and should be kept at a winter minimum of 7–10°C (45–50°F). *C. rhombifolia* needs similar conditions to *C. antarctica*, but has glossy dark green leaves composed of three leaflets, and forked tendrils. *C. discolor* is the rex begonia vine, so called because of its velvety leaves, which are dark green above with white bands between the veins, and mahogany red beneath. It is more tender, but makes a good house plant where it can be kept at 12–15°C (54–59°F) in winter. *C. striata* is hardier than any of these, needing only to be kept free of frost in winter. It is a vigorous yet elegant evergreen tendril climber, with leathery, lustrous, deeply cut leaves on zigzag stems that will grow to 9 m (30 ft) where it can range freely.

CLIMBERS FOR HOT, SUNNY WALLS

Several of the plants in the preceding section, such as *Tecomaria capensis*, can be grown on sunny walls in very mild gardens where winter frosts seldom or never occur. Those that follow, however, are on the whole hardy climbers; they need a good baking in summer, as we have seen, which will promote flowering.

Bignonia capreolata, the cross vine, from the south eastern United States, gets its name from the pattern shown in a cross-section of the stem. It is a very vigorous, evergreen tendril climber to 7.5 m (25 ft), with hooks or adhesive pads at the tips of the tendrils. The flowers are typical of the family, orange-scarlet trumpets with flared lobes, paler within, opening at mid summer. Propagate by spring cuttings with bottom heat.

The cat's claw vine, *Macfadyena unguis-cati* (*Doxantha unguis-cati*), has tiny hooks on its tendrils, as sharp and tenacious as a kitten's claws. The flowers are bignonia-style trumpets, bright yellow in colour, opening in late spring and summer. Increase by summer cuttings. It grows to 9 m (30 ft).

The trumpet vines or *Campsis* are in the bignonia family too. One grows wild in the same areas as *Bignonia capreolata*, the other comes from China. They flower in late summer and lose their ash-like leaves in winter. Increase by late summer cuttings. *C. grandiflora* is the Chinese species, a twining climber with large orange trumpets, the flared lobes paler peach to apricot-orange, in clusters. It reaches 9 m (30 ft). From North America comes *C. radicans*, a self-clinging climber with orange-tubed, scarlet-lobed trumpet flowers. Its paler form, 'Flava', has flowers of soft butter-yellow. Both grow to 12 m (40 ft). Perhaps the most suitable for cooler climates is *C. × tagliabuana* 'Madame Galen', a cross between the Chinese and the North American trumpet vines. It is spectacular in flower, with clusters of salmon-scarlet trumpets, and grows to 9 m (30 ft).

APPENDIX: CLIMBERS FOR SELECTED SITES AND QUALITIES

These lists have been prepared with cool–temperate climates in mind (equivalent to US Zones 6–8). For individual plants' requirements, see the main text. Gardeners in warmer climates will be able to add to these lists from the selection of conservatory climbers in Chapter 10.

Climbers for Full Sun

Actinidia deliciosa
  A. kolomikta
Bignonia capreolata
Campsis chinensis
  C. radicans
  C. × *tagliabuana*
Clematis armandii
  C. cirrhosa
  C. florida 'Sieboldii'
Jasminum

Lonicera etrusca
  L. splendida
Macfadyena unguis-cati
Passiflora
Podranea ricasoliana
Solanum
Tecomaria capensis
Vitis vinifera
Wisteria

Climbers for Shady Places

Adlumia fungosa
Akebia
Asteranthera ovata
Berberidopsis corallina
Celastrus orbiculatus
Clematis alpina
  C. macropetala
  C. montana
Clematis, many large-flowered varieties
Hedera
Hydrangea
Lapageria rosea
Lonicera × *americana*

  L. caprifolium
  L. periclymenum
  L. × *tellmanniana*
  L. tragophylla
Muehlenbeckia
Parthenocissus
Pileostegia viburnoides
Roses, many
(except in positions with overhead shade)
Schisandra
Schizophragma
Tropaeolum speciosum
Vitis coignetiae

Climbers for Restricted Spaces

Aconitum volubile
Adlumia fungosa
Anredera cordifolia
Asarina
Asteranthera ovata
Berberidopsis corallina
Billardiera
Bomarea
Clematis, some large-flowered hybrids
   C. texensis hybrids
Codonopsis
Euonymus fortunei varieties

Hedera helix, some varieties
Ipomoea
Kadsura japonica
Lablab purpureus
Lapageria rosea
Lathyrus
Mina lobata
Mutisia
Sollya
Thunbergia alata
Tropaeolum
Tweedia caerulea

Rampant Climbers Suitable for Large Spaces

Actinidia arguta
Celastrus orbiculatus
Clematis montana
Hedera colchica
Hydrangea petiolaris
Lonicera henryi
   L. japonica

Parthenocissus quinquefolia
   P. tricuspidata
Polygonum baldschuanicum
Rosa, synstylae (musk) group,
   species and hybrids
Vitis coignetiae
Wisteria

Climbers Suitable for Ground cover

Ampelopsis
Asteranthera ovata
Clematis × jouiniana
Decumaria
Ercilla volubilis
Euonymus fortunei varieties
Ficus
Hedera

Hydrangea
Lathyrus latifolius
Lonicera
Parthenocissus
Pileostegia
Schizophragma
Tropaeolum tuberosum
Vitis

Climbers for the Uprights of Pergolas

Actinidia kolomikta
   A. polygama
Billardiera longiflora
Clematis, large-flowered, especially
   Group 3 types of medium vigour
Euonymus fortunei varieties

Lonicera × brownii
   L. caprifolium
   L. periclymenum
Roses, several large-flowered climbers
Sollya

Climbers for Arches, Ropes, Chains and Pergola Cross-Beams

Aristolochia durior
Clematis montana
Jasminum officinale
Lonicera caprifolium
 L. periclymenum

L. tragophylla
Roses, rambler varieties
Rosa, synstylae species/hybrids
Vitis
Wisteria

Climbers that Flower for a Long Season
(including conservatory climbers)

Bougainvillea
Clematis, several large-flowered hybrids
 C. orientalis (*C. tibetana vernayi*) and
 varieties
 C. tangutica and varieties
Eccremocarpus scaber
Jasminum polyanthum
Lonicera 'Dropmore Scarlet'
Mandevilla laxa
Manettia inflata
Mina lobata

Passiflora caerulea
 P. × *caerulea-racemosa*
Plumbago auriculata
Rhodochiton atrosanguineum
Roses, many, especially large-flowered and
 Noisette/Tea-Noisette varieties
Solanum crispum 'Glasnevin'
 S. jasminoides
Sollya
Tropaeolum tuberosum 'Ken Aslet'

Self-Clinging Climbers

Asteranthera ovata
Campsis chinensis
 C. radicans
 C. × *tagliabuana*
Decumaria barbara
 D. sinensis
Ercilla volubillis
Euonymus fortunei varieties
Ficus pumila
Hedera

Hydrangea petiolaris
 H. serratifolia
Parthenocissus henryana
 P. quinquefolia
 P. tricuspidata
Pileostegia viburnoides
Schizophragma hydrangeoides
 S. integrifolia
Trachelospermum

BIBLIOGRAPHY

Bean, W. J. *Trees and Shrubs Hardy in the British Isles* 4 vols., 8th (revised) ed. John Murray, 1976–80

Bean, W. J. Supplement to 8th ed. John Murray, 1988

Bean, W. J. *Wall Shrubs and Hardy Climbers* Putnam, 1939

Beckett, Kenneth A. *Climbing Plants* Croom Helm, 1983

Fisk, J. *Clematis, the Queen of Climbers* Cassell, 1989

Fretwell, B. *Clematis* Collins, 1989

Grey-Wilson, Christopher & Matthews, Victoria *Gardening on Walls* Collins, 1983

Haworth-Booth, M. *The Hydrangeas* Garden Book Club, 1975

Hilliers' *Manual of Trees & Shrubs* David & Charles, 1972

Lloyd, Christopher & Bennett, T. H. *Clematis* Viking, 1989

Lucas Phillips, C. E. *Climbing Plants for Walls & Gardens* Heinemann, 1967

Rose, P. Q. *Climbers & Wall Plants* Blandford, 1982

Rose, P. Q. *Ivies* Blandford Press, 1980

Taylor, J. Kew Gardening Guides: *Climbing Plants* Collingridge, 1987

Thomas, G. S. *Climbing Roses Old & New* rev. ed. Dent, 1978

ACKNOWLEDGEMENTS

The photographs in this book are reproduced by kind permission of the following: p 2, 15, 22, 27, 46, 51 (top), 55, 59, 70, 78, 83, 86, 99, 102, 118 (bottom): Harry Smith Horticultural Photographic Collection; p 7, 10, 107: Pat Brindley; p 26, 74, 82, 98, 106: Jane Taylor; p 31, 51 (bottom), 67, 115: Andrew Lawson; p 118 (top): Sheila Orme; p 90, 95: Ward Lock.

INDEX